50 Top Birding Sites
in Kenya

Catherine Ngarachu

For my dear mother, Mary Chege,
who prays for all my dreams to come true.

Published by Struik Nature (an imprint of Penguin Random House South Africa (Pty) Ltd)
Reg. No. 1953/000441/07

The Estuaries No. 4, Oxbow Crescent (off Century Avenue), Century City, 7441 South Africa
PO Box 1144, Cape Town, 8000 South Africa

Visit **www.penguinrandomhouse.co.za** and join the Struik Nature Club for updates, news, events and special offers.

First published in 2017 by Struik Nature

10 9 8 7 6 5 4 3 2 1

Print 978 1 77584 248 4
ePub 978 177584 249 1
ePDF 978 177584 250 7

Publisher: Pippa Parker
Managing editor: Helen de Villiers
Editor: Emily Donaldson
Designer: Gillian Black
Cartographer: Liezel Bohdanowicz
Typesetter: Deirdré Geldenhuys
Proofreader: Thea Grobbelaar
Indexer: Sanet le Roux

Reproduction by Hirt & Carter Cape (Pty) Ltd
Printed and bound in Malaysia by Times Offset (M) Sdn Bhd.

Front cover photograph: Red-headed Weaver (Jacques Pitteloud)
Back cover photographs (anticlockwise, from top left): Storks and egrets at Amboseli (Peter Steward); Great White Pelicans (Peter Usher); Pygmy Falcons (Peter Usher); Sharpe's Longclaw (Jacques Pitteloud)
Title page photograph: Northern Red Bishop (Jacques Pitteloud)
Contents page: Mangrove Kingfisher (Peter Usher)

ACKNOWLEDGEMENTS

A very special thank you to the photographers Peter Usher, Jacques Pitteloud, Peter Steward, Dave Richards, Patrick L'Hoir, Paul Benson, Dino Martins and Wenfai Tong, who very generously shared the amazing and wonderful photos that enliven these pages – they are sure to inspire readers to get outdoors and watch birds.

I am so grateful to the individuals who reviewed one or more sites and kindly gave their insights, comments and suggestions. They are Ann Powys, Ben Mugambi (www.bensecologicalsafaris.com), Brian Finch, Colin Jackson, Darcy Ogada, David Fox, David J. Pearson, Dominic Kimani, Don Turner, Fleur Ng'weno, Joseph Kariuki (www.natureswonderlandsafaris.com), Kieran Avery, Lawrence Wagura, Marlene Reid, Martin Odino, Peter Mureithi, Peter Usher, Shailesh Patel, Tom Butyinski, Victor Olago, and Viktoria Schaule. I am also very grateful to Dino Martins and Gordon Boy for their generous contributions. This book is the better for the help and goodwill of those mentioned here, and any errors are entirely mine.

I also value and appreciate Nature Kenya – the East Africa Natural History Society and their willingness to support this book. I especially thank Fleur Ng'weno (honorary secretary of the Society) from whom I have learnt so much about birds over many years, Paul Matiku (executive director) for his encouragement, and the other members of staff, past and present, for their kind assistance. They include Brian Wambua, Emily Mateche, Francis Kagema, Fred Barasa, Jonathan Mwachongo, Serah Munguti, Simon Shati, and Washington Ayiemba.

Thank you also to all the many other fellow birders, guides, friends and colleagues who in various ways assisted and encouraged me, among them: Anastasia Mwaura, Ann and Ian Robertson, Ashah Owano (resource centre manager of National Museums of Kenya), Jagi Gakunju, Julia Fulcher, Kuria Waithaka, Leonard Ndungu, Luca Borghesio, Maaike Manten, Mike Davidson, Najma Dharani, Nancy Kinyanjui, Nani Croze, Ngugi Gechaga (corporate communications manager of Kenya Wildlife Service), Paul Buckley, Richard Barnley, Sukhy and Jaytinder Soin, Titus Imboma, Washington Wachira, Wendy Ayres, Werner Schroeder, and the committee of the Friends of City Park.

A huge thank you to my mother Mary, my sisters Elizabeth and Eunice, my brothers Frank and Stanley, and to Stanley's wife Lucy – there are not enough words to express my appreciation for your support.

Finally, thank you to all at Penguin Random House, in particular Pippa Parker for her enthusiasm in taking on this project and Emily Donaldson for her support and guidance.

Thank you all for helping to make this book happen.

Every day I look forward to observing the colours, sounds and habits of birds, and my hope is that this book will inspire a love of birds and motivate readers to go out and experience the diversity of birds, birding sites and habitats that make birding in Kenya so special.

Catherine Ngarachu
brilliantlycrafted.com

CONTENTS

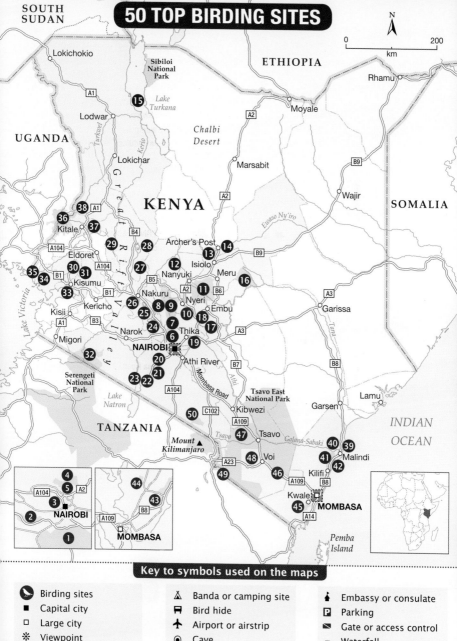

50 TOP BIRDING SITES

N

0 ——— 200
km

SOUTH SUDAN

Lokichokio

Sibiloi National Park

ETHIOPIA

Rhamu

A1

Lake Turkana

15

Lodwar

Chalbi Desert

Moyale

A2

UGANDA

Lokichar

Marsabit

B9

Wajir

SOMALIA

38 A1

36

Kitale

37

KENYA

A2

Ewaso Ny'iro

29

B4

28

Archer's Post

13

14

A104

Eldoret

A104

27

12

Isiolo

Meru

16

B9

35

30

31

Nanyuki

A2

B6

Garissa

34

B1

Kisumu

33

Kericho

B1

Nakuru

B5

26

8 **9**

11

Nyeri

Embu

A3

25

10

18

Tana

24

7

Thika

17

6

Narok

19

A3

Kisii

A1

B3

NAIROBI

Migori

20

Athi River

B7

32

21

22

Mombasa Road

23

A104

Athi

B8

Tsavo East National Park

Garsen

Lamu

Serengeti National Park

Lake Natron

Kibwezi

A109

Galana-Sabaki

TANZANIA

50

C102

47

Tsavo

40 **39**

INDIAN OCEAN

Mount Kilimanjaro

A23

48

Voi

41

Malindi

49

46

A109

Kilifi

42

B8

Kwale

45

MOMBASA

A14

Pemba Island

4

5 A2

3

A104

NAIROBI

2

1

44

43

A109

B8

MOMBASA

Key to symbols used on the maps

🐦 Birding sites	⛺ Banda or camping site		🛂 Embassy or consulate
■ Capital city	🛏 Bird hide		🅿 Parking
☐ Large city	✈ Airport or airstrip		✉ Gate or access control
✳ Viewpoint	⌂ Cave		= Waterfall
✕ Picnic site	✕ Restaurant		○ Spring
■ Other point of interest	▲ Highest peak		⑫ Path marker
♠ Accommodation	🎒 Information kiosk		\ Distance marker

The uncommon Verreaux's Eagle is seen soaring above rocky cliffs.

Kenya is the place for fantastic year-round birding and is considered one of the continent's must-visit birding destinations. The country currently boasts 1,060 different bird species – almost half the total number occurring in Africa.

On 30 November 1986, Terry Stevenson, John Fanshawe and Andy Roberts set a world record for spotting the greatest number of species within 24 hours: they logged 342 different bird species without using call recordings to attract them. Of these, 330 birds were actually seen, and not just heard. 'Big days' are not rare events – with some effort, birders may spot more than 80 species in a day's birding or 300 in a week. Some birding tours record over 800 species in less than a month of birding.

But numbers are just a small part of the bird-watching experience. The pastime mostly entails observing, learning about and enjoying birds in all their many colours, shapes and sizes. They are incredibly beautiful. They fly! Their songs and calls are among the best-loved sounds in nature. Birds also have distinct and fascinating behaviour and habits – their life history – and they have a way of becoming a life's passion.

Social weavers settle down for the night as the sun sets behind Mount Kenya.

Look for Little Grebe at wetlands with vegetation, including lakes, ponds and swamps.

One major reason why birding in Kenya is so productive is the country's wide diversity of habitats. Getting to know these habitats and the birds they support is what this book is all about. It introduces 50 of the most popular birding hot spots across eight different regions of the country, describing the species typically associated with them and helping prospective visitors to locate the sought-after 'specials' that may be found there.

The sites include well-known national parks and reserves, urban parks, private sanctuaries, a sewage pond, swamps, rice paddies, forests, lakes, museum sites and 'birdy' spots along major roads. Some are public facilities, others are private, some are freely accessible, many are accessible at a cost, but what they all have in common is birds!

To watch birds and see your bird list grow, it helps to have a field guide, a notebook and a pair of binoculars. Use this book to guide you to the best places to visit, and before you know it you'll be marvelling at the birds all around you.

The spectacular Lilac-breasted Roller is seen in grassland, acacia woodland and adjacent farmland.

Yellow-necked Spurfowl

Hunter's Sunbird

Intertidal wetlands

MAJOR BIRDING HABITATS IN KENYA

Not only is there a wide variety of habitats in Kenya, but often there is also a range of habitats within very close proximity at one site. Here we outline some of the major habitat types dealt with in this book and list typical bird species associated with each one. Note that certain birds are found across several habitat types, while others have a preference for just one habitat.

Intertidal wetlands

Intertidal wetlands are areas along the coastline that are submerged by the sea at high tide and exposed at low tide. Types of intertidal wetland include sand and mud flats and the remnants of the once extensive stretches of mangrove forests that grew along the eastern African shoreline. Typical birds include **Roseate Tern**, **White-fronted Plover**, **Mangrove Kingfisher** and Palaearctic migrants like **Ruddy Turnstone** and **Curlew Sandpiper**.

Coastal forest

Coastal forest

Coastal forests are among the most biologically important forests on the continent, owing to their high plant diversity and many endemic animal species. Birds typical of this habitat include **Fiery-necked Nightjar**, **Mombasa Woodpecker**, **Pale Batis**, **Chestnut-fronted Helmetshrike** and **Eastern Nicator**.

Semi-arid bushland

Most of the country is hot and dry for much of the year and is covered by vast expanses of open *Acacia* and *Commiphora* woodland. The thorn bush is occasionally interrupted where a river flows through it, or where isolated inselbergs or grass glades occur. Bushland-associated birds include **Vulturine Guineafowl**, **Lilac-breasted Roller**, **Von der Decken's Hornbill**, **D'Arnaud's Barbet** and **White-browed Sparrow Weaver**.

Semi-arid bushland

Alkaline lakes

The beautiful soda lakes of the Rift Valley in Kenya are highly saline, hostile environments, which are often fed by hot springs and rivers. Only specialized bird species can survive here. Examples include **Cape Teal**, **Greater** and **Lesser flamingos**, **Black-winged Stilt** and **Kittlitz's Plover**.

Alkaline lakes

Montane forest

Dry evergreen forests are found in the highlands and mountain ranges of central and western Kenya, and on the hillsides and mountains that tower over semi-arid plains in the north and south. The tree species growing in this habitat vary depending on the altitude and precipitation. Typical birds are **Narina Trogon, Montane Oriole, Grey Apalis, Yellow-whiskered Greenbul** and Palaearctic migrants like **Willow Warbler** and **Blackcap**.

Montane forest

Freshwater wetlands

Freshwater wetlands include lakes and swamps and may be permanent or seasonal. The quantity of water they hold varies according to the rainfall and other, often artificial, factors, such as water abstraction for irrigation. Typical freshwater wetland birds include **Yellow-billed Duck, Little Grebe, Black-crowned Night Heron, African Fish Eagle** and **Grey-headed Gull**.

Freshwater wetlands

Highland grasslands

Tussock grasses predominate in high-altitude grassland habitats. These regions are inhabited by a few specially adapted and rare animal species. Being largely unprotected, these grasslands are threatened by rapid changes in land use. **Cape Rook, Singing Cisticola, Common Stonechat, Northern Anteater Chat** and **Long-tailed Widowbird** are typical.

Highland grasslands

Grass plains

Grass plains

Also known as savanna, grass plains are found at mid- to low altitude and are characterized by grass expanses with a scattering of trees and riverine woodland. They are home to birds like **Common Ostrich**, **Secretarybird**, **Southern Ground Hornbill**, **Grassland Pipit** and Palaeartic migrants like **Red-backed** and **Lesser Grey shrikes**.

Semi-desert drylands

Water is scarce in these rocky drylands, and the animals found here are adapted to survive with little water. Vegetation comprises mainly low scrub and patchy grass, but greener foliage grows around springs and along riverbanks. Birds typical of this habitat include **Spotted Thick-knee**, **Crested Lark**, **Donaldson Smith's Sparrow Weaver**, **Black-capped Social Weaver** and **House Bunting**.

Rainforest

Kakamega Forest is the only remnant of rainforest in Kenya. The rainfall here may be as high as 1,700mm per year. The forest includes well-known African hard- and softwood trees, many shrubs and patches of grass. Some bird species that occur here include **Blue-headed Bee-eater**, **Chapin's Flycatcher** and **Turner's Eremomela**.

Semi-desert drylands

Rainforest

The Thrush Nightingale is a Palaearctic migrant that you might hear or see in a number of habitats east of the Rift Valley.

How to use this guide

This guide describes 50 selected birding sites around Kenya. To avoid repetition, little mention is made of the most common bird species that can be expected at many sites. According to Nature Kenya's Common Bird Monitoring programme, the following are the most frequently encountered species: **Speckled Mousebird**, **Red-eyed Dove**, **Hadada Ibis**, **Ring-necked Dove**, **Grey-backed Camaroptera**, **Baglafecht Weaver**, **Variable Sunbird**, **African Paradise Flycatcher**, **African Pied Wagtail**, **Tropical Boubou**, **Bronze Sunbird**, **Cattle Egret**, **Pied Crow**, **Streaky Seedeater**, **White-eyed Slaty Flycatcher** and **Augur Buzzard**. **Common Bulbul** is the most widespread bird species and **Red-billed Quelea** the most abundant. Vagrants and rarities also fall beyond the scope of this guide.

The bird names throughout this book follow the Fourth Edition of *Checklist of the Birds of Kenya* (2009).

Each site description includes the following elements:

- ■ **Key species:** Lists birds that are 'specials' at the site – species that birders are not likely to see elsewhere or that are easier to find here. They appear in **brown type** in the text. **Endemics** are indicated with a bracketed **(E)**. Some key species are passage migrants that travel through East Africa to overwinter in countries further south on the continent. For ease of reference, the order of key species listed follows the order of the *Checklist of the Birds of Kenya*. **IBA** is included in the heading when the site is classified as an 'Important Bird and Biodversity Area'. (See box p.12.)
- ■ **Introduction:** Describes where the site is located and why it is a birding hot spot.
- ■ **Habitat:** Outlines the physical features of the site and the predominant vegetation – both factors that are closely linked to the bird species that frequent the area.
- ■ **Getting there:** Gives directions to the birding site, always starting from the nearest large town or road.
- ■ **Visitor info:** Provides details that may help you to prepare for your visit, but is not exhaustive. Check the Internet for changes to entry fees and the like. Also see the useful links under 'Planning your visit', pp.15-17. Although we note whether overnight accommodation is available at the site, we do not endorse specific facilities, unless a lodge or camp is particularly relevant to the birding at that site. Internet links are provided where possible.
- ■ **The birding:** Introduces the common and notable birds likely to be encountered on a visit to the site, including those listed under 'Key species'. Also gives tips on where at the site you have the best chance of seeing a particular species and includes detailed site maps.
- ■ **Other wildlife:** Mentions other wildlife highlights at the site, where relevant.

Important Bird and Biodiversity Areas IBA

Thirty-two of the sites described in this book are Important Bird and Biodiversity Areas (IBAs), meaning that they are considered critical habitats for birds and other wildlife. They are designated, following globally agreed criteria, into one of four categories:

■ sites that hold globally threatened birds, such as **Taita Apalis** in the Taita Hills
■ sites that protect birds that live only in a very restricted range, such as **Sharpe's Longclaw**, which is found only in highland grasslands like those on the Kinangop Plateau
■ sites that hold large congregations of particular birds, such as **Lesser Flamingo** at Lake Bogoria, and
■ sites that hold species dependent on a particular ecosystem, like **Papyrus Gonolek** at Yala Swamp.

The IBA programme identifies, monitors and works to conserve sites that are important for birds. Nature Kenya, the East Africa Natural History Society, coordinates this programme in Kenya, working with its members, local community groups (called site support groups), Kenya Wildlife Service, Kenya Forestry Service, the National Environment Management Authority and other governmental and non-governmental organizations. Information on these sites can be found in *Important Bird Areas in Kenya*, a directory by Leon Bennun and Peter Njoroge, published by Nature Kenya in 1999.

A flock of Lesser Flamingos takes flight, while Greater Flamingos are seen in the distance.

Driving beyond Baragoi market town on a road trip to Lake Turkana

PLANNING YOUR VISIT

Birding trips to Kenya are generally very rewarding, due to the excellent bird guides, availability of tailored transport services and abundance of great accommodation. What follows are some helpful tips and background information for planning your visit.

Rainfall patterns

Kenya's traditional cycle of rains includes 'long rains' in March and April, 'short rains' in October and November, 'grass showers' in February and a scattering of 'Christmas rains' at the end of the year. Hail may occur along with the rain. These patterns vary locally: on the coast, the long and short rains may arrive a little later than in the rest of the country, while in the Lake Victoria basin afternoon showers can be a regular occurrence, especially in the wettest months of the year. Weather patterns have become less predictable than in the past, with rains often arriving earlier or later than expected and dry months being drier or wetter than anticipated.

If you are visiting during one of the rainy seasons, be prepared for muddy tracks. Also note that road and track conditions are more challenging when it rains and that in wilderness areas a four-wheel drive vehicle is recommended.

Average temperatures

In the cold season, which lasts from July to September, the days are typically cloudy and grey. Buildings are designed to be cool, and most of them lack heating, so it can get cold, especially at elevations above 1,500m. In the highlands particularly, night-time temperatures in the cold season can fall well below 10°C, rising by midmorning to just 14°C. Outdoors, if a wind picks up, it can feel colder. Fog and mist may also set in during the night.

The hottest and driest months in Kenya are December, January and February. The days are sunny, bright and hot even before you step out in the morning. At lower elevations, a cloudless day can range from 25°C to 28°C and may even exceed 30°C.

Jacques Pitteloud

The Grey Crowned Crane is a resident of many wetland areas, but its numbers are rapidly declining.

In between the hot and cold seasons, nights are often cool. The temperature on waking averages about 14°C and quickly warms up to highs of 25°C or more. Note that at the coast it is hot and humid for most of the year, with the coolest months being August and September.

Whatever time of year you visit, it's generally best to wear layers so that you can shed them as the day progresses and put them back on in the evenings.

Mosquitoes are prevalent in most places but less so at higher elevations, making malaria less of a concern here.

The best time for birding
Birds are seen throughout the year, so birding trips in Kenya can be rewarding at any time. The main considerations are travelling comfort and the accessibility of sites. In the wettest month (usually April), you may not wish to visit places that are prone to flooding or experiencing poor road conditions. You might, however, enjoy visiting after the rains, for example in May, when some flowering trees and plants are still in blossom and the landscape is beautifully green.

There are plenty of places to go for short birding trips too, and these may offer a welcome change. In the cold season, many birders in Nairobi relish a weekend in the warmer areas down Magadi Road (Site 20), for example.

The arrival of Palaearctic migrants in September and October swells the number of species that can be seen. If your aim is to see as many different birds as possible, then the hot months of December and January are the best time to go birding. But note that these months are the peak or 'high' season, when sites will be more crowded, and camps and lodges charge higher rates.

Birding is best in the cool hours of early morning and in the late afternoon, when the day's heat has started to dissipate.

Entering parks and reserves

Kenya Wildlife Service (KWS) is a governmental body entrusted with conserving and managing wildlife in Kenya. In this guide we have indicated which hot spots are managed by KWS. (See 'Visitor info' in the site descriptions.) These parks are open daily from 06h00 to 18h00, and KWS fees and rules apply. See www.kws.go.ke.

Until recently KWS parks would take cash or you had to present a Safari Card. A new system is being developed. KWS parks will now only accept direct bank deposits (Kenya Shillings or US dollars), credit card (Visa and Master Card), or mobile phone payments via the Safaricom M-Pesa (money transfer by mobile phone). Each park has its own M-Pesa paybill number, but it is best to pay on arrival at the park gate. All designated entry gates accept M-Pesa payments.

Fees are variable, depending on whether you are an East African citizen (from Burundi, Kenya, Rwanda, Tanzania or Uganda), an East African resident, or a visitor from another country. See www.kws.go.ke/content/park-fees-and-accommodation for the latest park fees and accommodation rates. Note also that to access KWS-managed wildlife areas you will need to present an identification card or passport if you are an East African citizen, or a work permit or alien card if you are a resident.

In most national parks and reserves you are required to remain in your vehicle. There are usually some picnic spots or viewing points (often with toilet facilities), where signage indicates that you can step out of your car – but do be careful. If you wish to walk down a designated nature trail, ask to be escorted by an armed ranger.

If you want to leave the park and then return later in the afternoon or the next morning on the same ticket, you should make your request to the warden at the gate before you exit. Ensure your details and those of your vehicle and passengers are noted. You can visit the KWS 'Frequently Asked Questions' page online for more information.

At many sites KWS works closely with the Kenya Forest Service (KFS), another governmental body, which is entrusted with conserving and managing the country's forest resources. Sites described in this book that are wholly or partly managed by KFS are Arabuko-Sokoke Forest, Karura Forest, Kakamega Forest and Mount Kenya. Currently the rates per person per day, where applicable, are KES 200 for Kenyan and East African community citizens, 400 for Kenyan residents and 600 for non-residents. KFS rates are now also paid by M-Pesa.

Reserves such as Samburu, Shaba and Masai Mara, which are partly or wholly managed by their local counties, follow similar rules and procedures to those applied in KWS-managed parks. However, they set their own tariffs and payment regulations.

The main entry gate to Shaba National Reserve

Finding local bird guides

Local bird guides are very good at locating and identifying the so-called 'specials', by sight and by call. They are often associated with local conservation groups known as site support groups (SSGs). The 'Visitor info' for each hot spot lists the contact details of local bird guide associations where applicable.

Some of these associations can also be contacted in advance of your trip via the offices of Nature Kenya in Nairobi. Email:
■ office@naturekenya.org for associations in the Mount Kenya (Naro Moru route), South Nandi and Gede areas, or
■ nkcoast@naturekenya.org for those associated with Arabuko-Sokoke Forest, Sabaki Estuary and Dakatcha Woodlands.

If you book a birding safari with a tour company, you can request a professional bird guide, if one is not already booked with the tour. Bird guides are also affiliated with some camps and lodges. A number of safari companies specializing in birding can be found by searching online.

Booking overnight accommodation

A site may have one or more of the following options available: camp sites (often the most budget-friendly option but requiring a good deal of self-sufficiency), self-catering bandas or guesthouses, which may be furnished, lodges and permanent tented camps.

At its parks and reserves Kenya Wildlife Service offers public and private camp sites, bandas and guesthouses, which are all self-catering (www.kws.go.ke/where-to-stay). The guesthouses and, increasingly, the bandas are equipped with bedding, utensils, cutlery and gas, but there are exceptions. It's best to enquire when you make reservations. Email reservations@kws.go.ke or marketing@kws.go.ke or call +254 (0) 726 610 533.

A growing number of relatively new budget to mid-range accommodation options including hotels, inns and guesthouses are springing up in towns around the country, which, where distances permit, may be preferable – enquire from your travel agent or search travel review websites online.

Visitors to the Kakamega Forest area can book to stay at the charming Rondo Retreat.

A Lanner Falcon with a swift that it has captured in the cliffs south of Lake Naivasha

HOW TO GET INVOLVED

If you wish to join other birders in their activities and to contribute your own birding records and observations, the following are some useful contacts:

■ **Nature Kenya:** Established in 1909, Nature Kenya (www.naturekenya.org) champions bird conservation in Kenya. It works to promote the study, enjoyment and conservation of nature. Members receive a copy of the annual birding magazine *Kenya Birding*, entry to national museum sites open to the public, and a monthly newsletter. It is a hub for birders and for many birding initiatives.

■ **Wednesday morning bird walks:** Participants meet at the Nairobi National Museum, just beyond the entrance to the galleries, at 08h30 on a Wednesday, and visit a different site in Nairobi each week. There is no charge for members of Nature Kenya, and temporary membership is available. E-mail **membershipservices@ naturekenya.org** for more information.

■ **Sunday Birdwatch:** Sunday Birdwatch meets at 09h00 on the third Sunday of each month at the Nairobi National Museum, just beyond the entrance to the galleries. Take binoculars and a picnic lunch. You should organize your own transport, if possible, as these outings normally take place outside of the city. E-mail **membershipservices@ naturekenya.org** for more information.

■ **Friends of City Park nature walks:** A guided walk is scheduled on the first Saturday of every month at City Park in Parklands, Nairobi. Many of the walks focus on birds, and anyone is welcome to attend. Email **cityparkfriends@ naturekenya.org** for more information.

■ **Mombasa bird walks:** Email the Friends of Fort Jesus at **ffjmsa@gmail. com** for information regarding bird walks in Mombasa.

■ **East African Rarities Committee**: If you have seen a rare bird, you can report to this committee by emailing **birds@ naturekenya.org**. They are responsible for vetting the first five records of a species for Kenya, along with other unusual records.

■ **Kenyabirdsnet:** This is a Yahoo Listserv where local subscribers can post interesting bird sightings and observations. To subscribe, email **kenyabirdsnet-subscribe@yahoogroups. com** or email **kenyabirdsnet@ yahoogroups.com** to post messages.

■ **Kenya Bird Map Project:** This project maps Kenya's bird species. It monitors changes in bird distribution and abundance to help determine conservation priorities and actions. Visit **kenyabirdmap. adu.org.za** to see the annual coverage of the project, current species distribution maps and to download data. Better still, email **kenyabirdmap@naturekenya.org** to join and contribute your own records.

SITE 1

NAIROBI NATIONAL PARK IBA

KEY SPECIES

African Finfoot, Shelley's Francolin, Madagascar Pond Heron, White-backed Night Heron, Secretarybird, White-backed Vulture, Hartlaub's Bustard, Grey Crowned Crane, Brown-backed Woodpecker, White-tailed Lark, Siffling Cisticola, Jackson's Widowbird, Nairobi Pipit (a known but undescribed species). **Passage migrants**: Red-backed Shrike, Whinchat.

Nairobi National Park is remarkable in that it is a wild game park situated alongside a city. Indeed, housing increasingly surrounds its southern boundary, which previously was largely open to the Athi-Kapiti Plains. The park, which is situated at an altitude of 1,780–1,500m, is 117km² in area, 24km at its widest point, and encompasses a wealth of contrasting habitats. As a result, the bird list runs to 520 species, of which 200 can often be recorded in a single day, especially 'in season', that is, when Palaearctic migrant birds are present, from October to April.

HABITAT

The park includes open grassland and lightly wooded plains, with rocky valleys, seasonal swamps, dams, forest-lined rivers and streams, and – along its western boundary – a thin strip of upland forest. The open grassland is scattered with *Acacia* and *Balanites aegyptiaca* trees and with delightful wild flowers that come out with the rains. These include the white and pink blossoms of *Cycnium* spp., which resemble strewn tissue paper, the bright yellow flowers of *Hypoxis obtusa* and the pink rosettes of *Ammocharis tinneana*. The dry, evergreen, upland forest is dominated by *Croton megalocarpus* and *Schrebera alata* to the west and by *Brachylaena hutchinsii* and African olive *Olea europaea* subsp. *cuspidata* to the east.

GETTING THERE

The park's Main Gate is 8km southwest of the city centre, on the Langata Road. Three of the other gates – East Gate, off Mombasa Road, Maasai Gate, leading out to the south, and Langata Gate, in the forest to the west of Magadi Road – can be used for entry or exit.

VISITOR INFO

Nairobi National Park is managed by Kenya Wildlife Service and an entry fee is payable. You will need to present identification. Bring a picnic breakfast and get an early start. At some sites baboons may be a problem, but you can usually find an undisturbed spot. If they are present keep your windows closed. The only accommodation available in the park is at the Nairobi Tented Camp (**www. nairobitentedcamp.com**), but to the south, adjoining the park, there are a number of overnight options including Maasai Lodge (**www.maasailodge.com**) and the Silole Sanctuary (**www. silolesanctuary.com**).

Madagascar Pond Heron

Peter Steward

THE BIRDING

From the Main Gate, the road descends through *Croton* forest to the plains. A left turn at the first junction leads to the Ivory Burning Site, where, in 1989, a 12-tonne stack of elephant tusks was burned in protest against the ivory trade. This is now a picnic area surrounded by scrub and a few acacias. In season (October–April), it is worth making an early morning stop here for common and uncommon migrants, including **Eurasian Bee-eater**, **Upcher's** and **Willow warblers**, **Blackcap**, nightingales and **Irania**. Also look low down in the surrounding scrub for **Crested** and **Scaly francolins**.

African Moustached Warbler

The Hyena Dam is a permanent pond with an exposed mudbank and marshy overflow areas, often extensively covered with bulrushes. On the mudbank you may see **Spur-winged Goose**, **Red-billed** and **Hottentot teals** and **Blacksmith** and **Long-toed plovers**. **Common Greenshank**, **Green** and **Wood sandpipers** and **Yellow Wagtail** are often seen feeding here between October and March. Watch the bulrushes patiently, and **Little Bittern, Madagascar Pond Heron** (Malagasy migrant, May–September), **African Water Rail, Purple Swamphen** or **Allen's Gallinule** may make an appearance. Scan the marshes near the dam for **Saddle-billed Stork**, and check for raptors in the large acacia across the way from the viewing area.

Most of the park consists of undulating open plains with red or black cotton soils that support grasses. As you drive, watch out for movement: larks and pipits are numerous, most commonly **Rufous-naped Larks** and flocks of **Somali Short-toed Larks**. Waxbills and **Cinnamon-breasted Bunting** may also be feeding on the road. From October to April, **Red-backed Shrike** and **Whinchat** hunt from the tops

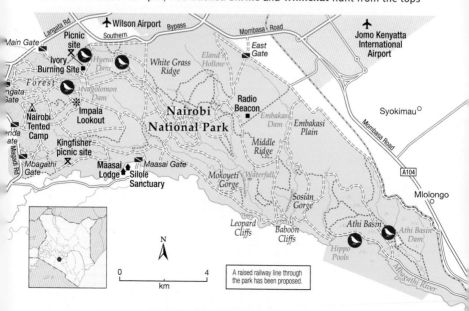

A raised railway line through the park has been proposed.

of bushes, while **Isabelline** and **Northern wheatears** are often seen on the ground. **Stout**, **Zitting**, **Desert** and **Pectoral-patch cisticolas** call in display flights over grass and low bushes.

When the grass is tall after the rains (May–July), **White-winged**, **Red-collared**, and **Jackson's widowbirds** are conspicuous in their beautiful breeding plumage. When the grass is shorter, **Harlequin Quail**, **Spotted Thick-knee**, **Black-winged Plover** and **Temminck's Courser** are easier to see. **Secretarybird** may be spotted striding in the distance, while bustards often stand looking curiously about before marching off. It is not unusual to see **Tawny** and **Martial eagles** on the top of a *Balanites* tree, **Black-shouldered Kite** hovering, **Lesser Kestrel** and **Amur Falcon** flying through the area in season, and **harriers** quartering the plains in search of prey, all in a single morning.

The Athi Basin comprises scrub grassland with rocky outcrops. Here, **Shelley's Francolin**, hard to find elsewhere in Kenya, feeds on the road in the early mornings and late afternoons. **African Quailfinch** and stunning **Pangani** and **Rosy-breasted longclaws** may also be seen feeding among the roadside grasses.

The Athi Dam is a magnet for waders when its margins are not submerged. Look for **Black-winged Stilt**, **Kittlitz's Plover**, and, from October to April, **Little Stint** and sandpipers (as well as huge resident crocodiles!). At the same time of year, **Red-throated Pipit** can be common in low scrub near the dam's northern edge, and **Black Stork** may stop to feed in small numbers.

At the Hippo Pools rangers are often available, and you can at last step from your vehicle and take a guided walk beside the Mbagathi River. Under large yellow fever trees *Acacia xanthophloea* the shy **African Finfoot** may be seen swimming in the early mornings. **White-backed Night Heron** and **Striated Heron** are resident, but skulk in thick cover during the day. **White-backed Vulture** nest in taller trees, while **Vitelline Masked Weaver** nests dangle from overhanging branches. **African Firefinch** and **Black-faced Waxbill** may flit about low in the scrub. Also look for kingfishers (including **Grey-headed** and **Striped**), **Green-backed Honeybird**, **Red-throated Tit**, warblers (including **African Moustached Warbler**) and seed-eating birds. Squads of **African Palm** and **Little swifts**, **Plain** and **Banded martins** may rush through on their rapid precision flights.

The open meadows at the forest edge on the climbing road to the Impala Lookout are where the **Nairobi Pipit** is most easily located, flying into trees when flushed. Here also, **Siffling Cisticola** is perhaps the commonest bush bird. Further along this road mixed flocks in the forest usually include **White-bellied Tit**, but may also yield the rare **Brown-backed Woodpecker**.

Giraffe in the grasslands near the northern edge of the park

OTHER WILDLIFE

Regardless of the time of year you are almost always likely to see zebra, Thomson's and Grant's gazelles, impala, giraffe, warthog, Coke's hartebeest and wildebeest. Lion, eland, both white and black rhinos, waterbuck and buffalo are also resident.

NGONG ROAD FOREST SANCTUARY

KEY SPECIES
Ayres's Hawk Eagle, Crowned Eagle, Narina Trogon, Brown-backed Scrub Robin, White-starred Robin.

Less than 10km from Nairobi, adjacent to the Ngong Racecourse, lies what remains of a once vast upland forest. The 538ha Ngong Road Forest Sanctuary is a good place to see many birds including **Crowned Eagle**, **Narina Trogon** and **White-starred Robin**, without having to venture too far from the city.

HABITAT
Trees in the Ngong Forest include African olive *Olea europaea* subsp. *africana*, figs *Ficus* spp., pencil cedars *Juniperus procera*, known locally as *mutarakwa*, and many other Nairobi garden favourites, including *Albizia schimperiana*, *Warburgia ugandensis*, *Craibia brownie*, *Schrebera alata* and magnificent yellow-flowered *Ochna* spp. *Eucalyptus* and acacias also cover large areas.

GETTING THERE
From Dagoretti Corner on Ngong Road, Nairobi, it is about 2km to the Ngong Forest Sanctuary. Bear left towards the suburb of Karen, passing the Jamhuri Park Showground and Nairobi Polo Club. Turn left at the sign for the Main Gate of the Ngong Road Forest Sanctuary. Travel 800m up the Ngong Road to reach the Ngong Racecourse.

VISITOR INFO
The Ngong Road Forest Association (**www. ngongforest.org**) manages the forest, which has recently been split into five sections by the new Southern Bypass. Contact the association office at **office@ngongforestsanctuary.com** to arrange a guide who will walk you around for a modest fee. Be cautious if entering the forest without a guide – do not carry valuables, and do not go alone.

Narina Trogon

Paths provide openings in the forest for birding.

Yellow-billed Duck

THE BIRDING

That part of the forest's edge overlooking the racecourse offers opportunities to see raptors as well as swifts and swallows. In particular, this is a good place to see **Ayres's Hawk Eagle** and **African Cuckoo Hawk** (an Afrotropic migrant), along with various migrant birds of prey flying overhead in season.

A number of tracks give access to the indigenous Ngong Forest, between broad avenues used by local equestrians. There is an active **Crowned Eagle** nest, which the forest guide will be able to show you. **White-starred Robin** and pairs of **Hartlaub's Turaco** and **Narina Trogon** can usually be found within patches of dense woodland, and, after rain, the dazzling **Emerald Cuckoo** can generally be heard, if not seen. A variety of **greenbuls** (including **Yellow-whiskered and Cabanis's**, and sometimes the scarce **Yellow-bellied**, too) often leave the cover of the forest to take advantage of abundant fruiting trees at the forest's edge, where they mingle with foraging doves, tinkerbirds and starlings.

On a dam at the forest's edge near the entrance to the racecourse, **African Black** and **Yellow-billed ducks** are quite often present. In the *Lantana* scrub around this dam, look for **Singing Cisticola**, **Dark-capped Yellow Warbler** and **Brown-backed Scrub Robin**.

OTHER WILDLIFE

As unlikely as it seems in the city, hyena and bushbuck tracks are sometimes seen.

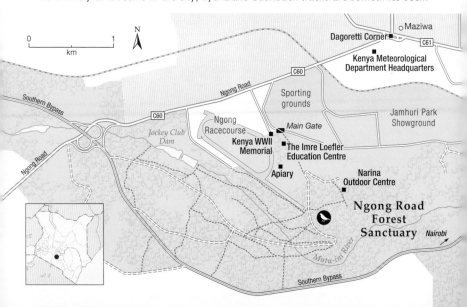

NAIROBI ARBORETUM

KEY SPECIES
African Black Duck, African Goshawk, Hartlaub's Turaco, Lesser Honeyguide, African Paradise Flycatcher, Cabanis's Greenbul, Mountain Wagtail and many sunbirds.

The Nairobi Arboretum is a pleasant 30ha open woodland with many trails and is bounded to the north by the Kirichwa Kubwa River. It was established in 1907 as a place to test out fast-growing trees, because a ready supply of wood was needed to fuel the steam engines running on the recently completed Kenya–Uganda railway line.

HABITAT
The seeds planted in the Arboretum were sourced from around the country and the world. You will find a glorious display of local and exotic trees, including the bunya-bunya *Araucaria bidwillii* and Brewster's cassia *Cassia brewsteri* from Australia, tipa *Tipuana tipu* from Bolivia and the Indian rubber tree *Ficus elastica*. Today, this wide range of indigenous and exotic trees and shrubs provides highland birds with flowers and fruit almost year-round.

GETTING THERE
The main entrance to the Arboretum is less than 2km from Nairobi's University Way roundabout, off Uhuru Highway. Take State House Road past the university residences, and, being careful of oncoming traffic, turn right into Arboretum Drive, a cul-de-sac leading to the Arboretum's car park and main entrance. About 80m before the main gate you'll see a track with a signpost reading 'Grounds for hire'. Take this route to reach the visitors' centre, which is known as the Tree Centre.

VISITOR INFO
The Arboretum is open between 06h00 and 18h15 daily. Individuals have to pay an entry fee at the main entrance, and parking is available at a modest price. Visit the Friends of Nairobi Arboretum (nairobiarboretum.org) office at the Tree Centre, which is open on weekdays between 09h00 and 16h00, for information about monthly tree walks, group visits and other events. You can also purchase a birding checklist or the guidebook *Nairobi Arboretum – the place of trees*. For birding, the Arboretum is best avoided on Sundays and public holidays, as it can be crowded.

The rufous morph of African Paradise Flycatcher; white morphs are more common in the drier parts of the country.

Yellow-whiskered Greenbul

THE BIRDING

Green-backed Honeybird, African Paradise and **White-eyed Slaty flycatchers, Black-backed Puffback, Tropical Boubou, Tawny-flanked Prinia, Olive Thrush, Collared, Amethyst,** and **Bronze sunbirds, Baglafecht Weaver, Red-billed Firefinch** and **Bronze Mannikin** are some of the typical Nairobi garden birds that can be found among the trees and scrub and in the more open areas of the Arboretum. Listen for a **Lesser Honeyguide** calling from the canopy of a tall tree, and look for an **Augur Buzzard,** soaring or perched.

Some uncommon visitors include **Silvery-cheeked Hornbill,** various starlings and, in season (October–April), **Eurasian Bee-eater, Willow Warbler, Blackcap** and **Grey Wagtail.**

Walk along the pathways above the river, where there are forested slopes. Here, and wherever the tree cover is thick, you may see **African Goshawk, Little Sparrowhawk, Hartlaub's Turaco, Narina Trogon** and **Rüppell's Robin Chat.** (A lone **Purple-crested Turaco** also took up residence in the Arboretum in the 2010s.) The *It-will-rain* call of the large **Red-chested Cuckoo** resonates before and during the rainy season, but like the **Yellow-whiskered, Grey-olive** (rare) and **Cabanis's greenbuls,** this species is not often seen.

On the riverside walk, look out for a resident pair of **African Black Duck,** as well as **Hamerkop, Malachite Kingfisher** and **Mountain Wagtail.**

Common city birds that you are likely also to see at the Arboretum are **Marabou Stork, Sacred Ibis, Black Kite, Little Swift, Pied Crow** and **African Pied Wagtail.**

OTHER WILDLIFE

Mole-rats are hunted by the raptors, while vervet and Sykes's monkeys may try to grab your picnic. The Arboretum is also home to the four-toed hedgehog, squirrels, chameleons and a large variety of butterflies and other insects.

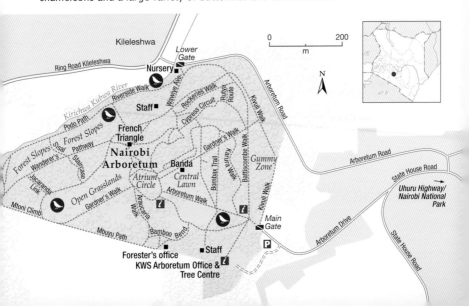

KARURA FOREST RESERVE

KEY SPECIES

Long-crested Eagle, African Crowned Eagle, Narina Trogon, Yellow-whiskered Greenbul, Slender-billed Greenbul, Cabanis's Greenbul and Brown-chested Alethe.

Karura Forest is a large expanse (about 1,000ha) of indigenous, dry, evergreen forest with patches of plantation, located in the northern suburbs of Nairobi. More than 160 highland, forest and wetland bird species have been recorded here.

HABITAT

The forest is in a part of Nairobi with hills and valleys, grassy meadows and marshy areas. Distinctive trees in the indigenous forest are labelled, including the *muthiga* or East African greenheart *Warburgia ugandensis*, silver oak *Brachylaena huillensis*, known locally as *muhuhu*, forest newtonia *Newtonia buchananii* and Nile tulip *Markhamia lutea*. The plantation comprises large old stands of eucalyptus (which are being replaced), *Cupressus* spp., *Grevillea robusta* and monkey puzzle *Araucaria columnaris* trees.

GETTING THERE

You can access the reserve via any of the gates, but the main entry is in Limuru Road, not far from the Muthaiga Shopping Centre and diagonally opposite the Belgian Embassy. An additional gate, Gate C or 'Shark's Gate', has recently been opened so that visitors can access the eastern part of the forest.

Peter Steward

Watch out for the amazing scarlet coloration of the wings, visible when Hartlaub's Turaco takes flight.

Common Moorhen

VISITOR INFO

The forest is open daily from 06h00 to 17h30. You will need to pay an entry fee at the gate, where you can also purchase a map and a leaflet about the birds. From the main gate in Limuru Road it is just over a kilometre to the Karura Forest Environmental Education Trust (KFEET) Centre. You can choose to park and start walking the trail from the Limuru Gate or, for a small extra fee, drive up the hill, park at the KFEET Centre and start

THE BIRDING

The trail is 5km in total and takes you through exotic woodlands, indigenous forest, along the Karura River and past Lily Lake. Look out for **Tambourine Dove**, **Yellow-rumped Tinkerbird** and **White-bellied Tit** as you walk through the plantation woodlands before and beyond the KFEET Centre. Unlikely as it seems, escaped **African Grey Parrots** have adapted to this part of the city and are occasionally seen.

Lantana and *Tithonia* scrub grows at the edge of the road that goes past the KFEET Centre. Here, just beyond the security barrier and behind the scrub is a sedge-filled swampy area. **Long-crested Eagle**, **Grey-capped Warbler** and sunbirds are often seen here, while above the road there may be **Black Saw-wing**, **Plain Martin** and **Lesser Striped Swallow**.

Beyond this point the main junctions on the trails are numbered, so at the no.12 board take the path to the right. As the *Eucalyptus* and *Araucaria* trees give way to indigenous forest, you are likely to hear **Hartlaub's Turaco**, **Chin-spot Batis** and **Yellow-whiskered** and **Cabanis's greenbul**. **Narina Trogon** favour the 150m downhill track between boards 19 and 25.

Walk east of boards 24 and 25, where there is ideal forest habitat in which to look for **Klaas's** and **African Emerald cuckoos**, **Silvery-cheeked Hornbill** (seasonal), **Green-backed Honeybird**, **Black-backed Puffback**, **Yellow-whiskered**, **Slender-billed** and **Cabanis's greenbuls** and **Montane White-eye**. Scan for **African Black Duck** in the river above the waterfalls (near junction 26).

Walking past the junction board for trail 24 brings you within viewing

Long-crested Eagle

the trail from here. Professor Wangari Maathai, founder of the Green Belt Movement and the 2004 Nobel Peace Prize Laureate, played a key role leading residents in the struggle to keep Karura a public green space. Karura Forest is now one of the best recreational facilities in the city and is well utilized by thousands of residents, especially for walking, jogging and cycling.

A trail winds past some *Araucaria columnaris* trees.

distance of the nest of an **African Crowned Eagle**. Look a little above eye level in the trees at the Karura River's edge. Along this route you may also spot **Brown-chested Alethe** foraging in the leaf litter or perching on low twigs.

From here head for Lily Lake, which may have some open water, weeds, water lilies and mace reed *Typha* spp. Resident birds to look out for here include **White-backed** and **Yellow-billed ducks**, **Little Grebe**, **Common Moorhen**, **Malachite** and **Pied kingfishers**, and, between October and April, **Willow Warbler**, **Blackcap** and **Common Nightingale**. Lily Lake can also be reached by turning right out of the KFEET Centre.

OTHER WILDLIFE

Most conspicuous are Sykes's monkey, Harvey's duiker and suni. There are also the introduced black-and-white colobus monkeys, which seem to have taken very well to their new home.

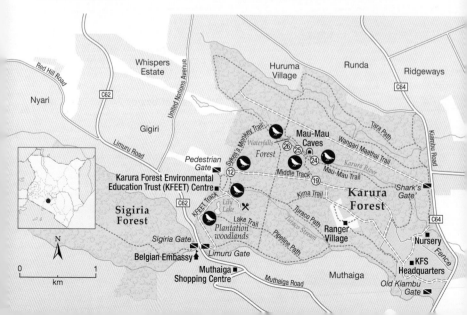

CITY PARK, NAIROBI

KEY SPECIES
Silvery-cheeked Hornbill, White-headed Barbet, Black Cuckooshrike, Slender-billed Greenbul and many sunbirds.

Although it is just 3km from Nairobi's central business district, City Park offers surprisingly rich birding. First set aside in the 1930s, it is a small remnant of upland forest with a river flowing through it. These days it comprises 60ha and includes gardens, lawns, historical cemeteries and a maze (called *Mtego Wa Panya*). Fruiting trees, flowers and other plants attract foraging monkeys, insects, amphibians and more than 120 highland bird species.

HABITAT
City Park slopes very gently down to the Kibagare River. It boasts many fine tree species, some familiar and others unfamiliar to this high-altitude region of Nairobi (1,600–1,800m). The formal areas include many *Bauhinia* spp., Nile tulip *Markhamia lutea*, with its clusters of bright yellow flowers, tall and graceful *Croton megalocarpus*, known locally as *mukinduri*, and Cape chestnut *Calodendron capensis*. Some landmark features are the jacaranda tree *Jacaranda mimosifolia*, which bears white, rather than lilac, flowers in October and November, the lianas and some amazing bougainvilleas, which scramble over trees or are pruned into tree-like shapes.

GETTING THERE
The main entrance to City Park is off Limuru Road, across from the Aga Khan Hospital (on your right if you are heading out of Nairobi), but before the entrance to the Hawkers' Market. Follow the road from the park's entrance, which passes the administration building and nurseries. There is a parking lot opposite the office building.

VISITOR INFO
City Park is a county facility and a national monument that is open to the public throughout the year. Bear in mind that this is an urban park and exercise caution, especially in the less frequented part of the park. Do not take valuables, and do not go alone, especially if you are carrying camera equipment. You can request a guide from the Friends of City Park (**friendsofcitypark.org**), a group that, for two decades, has protected this park from appropriation by developers. The many Sykes's monkeys at City Park are habituated to people and are likely to raid your picnic if they see or sense it. A guidebook *City Park – the Green Heart of Nairobi* is available at national museums.

Baglafecht Weaver

Peter Usher

THE BIRDING

A good starting point is the *Tithonia* scrub behind the parking lot, where there may be **Singing Cisticola, Dark-capped Yellow Warbler** and **Pin-tailed Whydah. Hadada Ibis** may be walking on the central grass, while **Amethyst, Bronze** or **Variable sunbirds** may be spotted in the low trees.

Look in the palm trees to the sides of the administration building for **African Palm Swift**, and check the power lines for resting **Lesser Striped Swallow**. Walk down the broad footpath left of the car park between tall *Casuarinas* towards the Bowling Green Restaurant, listening out for doves, **Black-backed Puffback, White-bellied Tit** and **Cape** and **Rüppell's** robin chats.

The neglected City Park cemetery is quiet and a great spot for **African Green Pigeon, White-headed Barbet, Yellow-rumped Tinkerbird, Cardinal** and **African Grey woodpeckers, Sulphur-breasted Bushshrike** and **Black Cuckooshrike**.

Make your way back to the central lawns. This is the busiest part of the park, but the beautiful flowering trees still manage to attract bee-eaters and sunbirds (commonly **Collared, Amethyst** and **Scarlet-chested**). Passing overhead there may be raptors like **Common Buzzard** (October–April) and the large, noisy **Silvery-cheeked Hornbill**, which is particularly conspicuous when trees are fruiting.

A number of bridges give access, via remnant forest, to the quieter, western side of the park. Listen out for **Yellow-whiskered, Slender-billed** and **Cabanis's greenbuls**. You will emerge at the maze, surrounded by glades and unkempt garden. Look for **Grey-headed Kingfisher, Chin-spot Batis, Abyssinian** and **Montane white-eyes, African Dusky Flycatcher, Baglafecht Weaver** and, from October to April, **Willow Warbler, Blackcap** and **Common Nightingale. Great Sparrowhawk** have nested here, and **Grey** (in season) and **Mountain wagtails** may be seen at the river's edge.

OTHER WILDLIFE

City Park is known for its monkeys and squirrels. See some of the park's butterfly diversity at the Butterfly House at the Boscowen Collection.

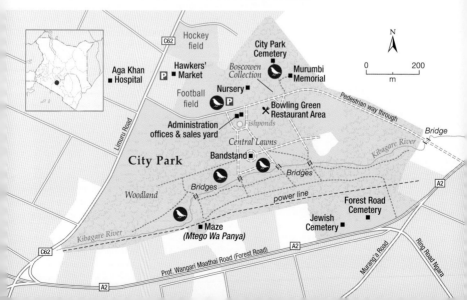

SITE 6

MANGUO POND, LIMURU

KEY SPECIES
White-backed Duck, Maccoa Duck, Augur Buzzard, Lesser Moorhen. **Passage migrants**: Northern Shoveler, Garganey.

Manguo Pond is a shallow seasonal wetland situated beside a major highway in a highland area. The water level may get very low, and the pond may even disappear in consecutive drought years. At other times, the basin may be full of water, with a spectacular array of ducks and migrating waders.

HABITAT
Manguo Pond is about 1km in length, half that in width, and is surrounded by human activity. It consists of roughly three parts – a drier floodplain in the north (which often hosts local football matches), marshy areas with *Cyperus* spp. and bulrushes in the south, and open water with some pondweed and floating sedge.

GETTING THERE
The pond is just off the A104 highway from Nairobi – a distance of about 35km, near the town of Limuru. Stay on the highway until you pass under the Limuru flyover and can see the pond on your right. Being careful of oncoming traffic, turn in and park at any spot along the pond's margin. To avoid the glare on sunny mornings, rather than turning in and parking on your right, keep left and go around and over the flyover, crossing to the opposite side of the pond.

VISITOR INFO
Limuru is notoriously cold, especially in the early mornings and in July and August, when temperatures may drop below 10°C. If there's wind, fog or mist it may feel colder still. Even when conditions are sunny, you should be prepared for the cold if you plan to stop for any length of time. The swamp is open to all, and there is no access fee. Be cautious with valuables, and keep an eye on your car.

The best time of year to visit is in April and May when there is breeding activity, and from October to April, when Palaearctic migrants are likely to be present. Note, however, that the water level can get very low.

Flocks of White-faced Whistling Ducks are common at wetlands around the country.

THE BIRDING

There are no tracks around the narrow fringes of the swamp, but you can get reasonable views from both sides. Look on the open water for the dark head and blue bill of the **Maccoa Duck**, a rare species that is a regular here. Other ducks include **White-backed** and **Fulvous Whistling ducks** (both of which breed here), **Hottentot Teal** and **Southern Pochard**. Large numbers of **White-faced Whistling Duck** may occur. From October to April, look among the ducks for **Northern Shoveler**, **Northern Pintail** and **Garganey**.

The open water is also likely to hold **Little Grebe**, **Lesser Moorhen** (an Afrotropic migrant), **Red-knobbed Coot** and, striding across floating mats of pondweed, **African Jacana**.

African Jacana

Partially concealed in islands of vegetation there may be **Little Bittern** and **Black-crowned Night Heron**; also look for the endangered **Madagascar Pond Heron** (a Malagasy migrant, June–September), **Purple Swamphen**, **Greater Painted-snipe** and **Lesser Swamp Warbler**.

Look to the northern edge of the pond where, from September to April, **Glossy Ibis**, **Marsh Sandpiper**, **Little Stint** and **Ruff** may be seen feeding in the mud, with **Yellow** (in season) and **Cape wagtails** and **Red-throated** (uncommon migrant) and **Grassland pipits** in the grass beyond. The trees on the east side of the pond may hold **Cape Rook**, **Common Stonechat**, sunbirds (**Bronze**, **Malachite**, **Golden-winged**), and weavers. Look in the skies above for **Western Marsh** and **Pallid harriers** (in season), **Augur Buzzard**, **Whiskered Tern** and **Plain Martin**.

OTHER WILDLIFE

Surprisingly, given how busy the location is, the Cape clawless otter has been seen here.

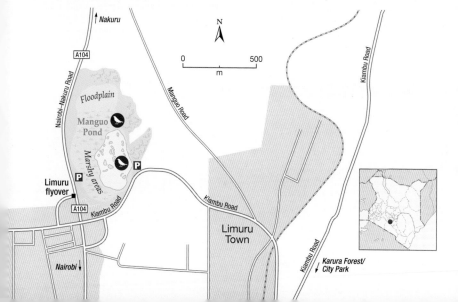

GATAMAIYU FOREST IBA

KEY SPECIES

Mountain Buzzard, Bar-tailed Trogon, Fine-banded Woodpecker, Black-fronted Bushshrike, White-tailed Crested Flycatcher, Evergreen Forest Warbler, Abbott's Starling, Brown-chested Alethe, Abyssinian Crimsonwing.

Gatamaiyu Forest is a segment of the Kikuyu Escarpment Forest, which lies at an altitude of 1,800–2,400m, on the southern slopes of the Aberdare range. Though surrounded by tea plantations and intensive farming, Gatamaiyu nonetheless offers some of the best highland-forest birding in the country.

HABITAT

This evergreen forest consists of many trees and shrubs including *Podocarpus* conifers, East African camphor wood *Prunus africana* and wild banana *Ensete* *ventricosum*. The Gatamaiyu River flows down a valley close to offices and a camp site of the Department of Fisheries. Growing alongside it are magnificent spiny tree ferns *Cyathea manniana*.

GETTING THERE

To reach Gatamaiyu Forest from Nairobi, take the A104 highway towards Naivasha. About 14km beyond the Limuru turn-off and 1km before reaching the town of Kimende, take the road to the left. This road arcs to the right and passes back under the highway.

Found at a wide range of sites, the Cardinal Woodpecker is one of the most common woodpeckers.

Jacques Pitteloud

As you emerge from beneath the highway you soon reach a T-junction, where you should turn right and then next left at St Peter The Rock Catholic Church. Follow this road and cross an intersection. Where the road forks, continue straight onto the road that skirts the electric fence at the forest's edge. You'll then reach some tea fields: continue straight, going over a steep rise, until you reach a small bridge over the Gatamaiyu River. Cross it and climb the next hill. At the top, take the left-hand track. Proceed along the narrow road between the farm fences for about 1km and go through the gate. The office of the Gatamaiyu Fishing Camp is just a little further on, to the left.

VISITOR INFO

A modest fee, payable at the camp, allows you to park or picnic. The forest is inhabited by elephants – watch and listen out for them, and beware of stinging nettles alongside the tracks. For a local guide contact Kijabe Environment Volunteers (kenvo-kenya.com).

THE BIRDING

The Gatamaiyu Fishing Camp is a good place to start. On the weedy grass you may find **Lemon Dove** and waxbills. (If you camp here overnight you might also hear **African Wood Owl** and **Montane Nightjar**.) Search the trees around the camp site clearing and the entry barrier. Birds typical of this forest include **Scaly-throated Honeyguide, Fine-banded** and **Cardinal woodpeckers, White-bellied Tit, White-browed Crombec, White-eyed Slaty Flycatcher, Green-headed, Amethyst** and **Northern Double-collared** sunbirds, **Spectacled and Brown-capped weavers** and **Yellow-crowned Canary**. A mixed party passing through can include **Moustached Tinkerbird, Montane Oriole** and the range-restricted and uncommon **Abbott's Starling.**

Peter Usher

Northern Double-collared Sunbird

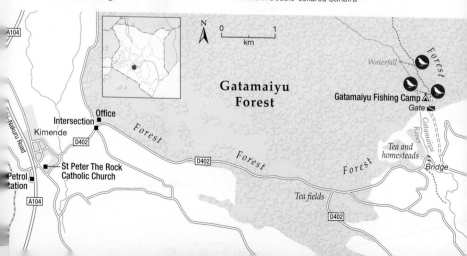

Cape Robin Chat

Watch the forest track ahead for **Scaly Francolin** and look for **Brown-chested Alethe** on the ground alongside it. You may hear the calls of **Cape** and **Rüppell's robin chats** or those of the similar-sounding **African Hill Babbler**.

Cinnamon Bracken and **Evergreen Forest warblers** are great skulkers and inhabit the undergrowth, where you are also likely to come upon the beautiful **Black-collared Apalis** and **Abyssinian Crimsonwing**. Other apalises (**Grey, Chestnut-throated** and **Black-throated**) and warblers (**Mountain Yellow** and **Brown Woodland**) and – from October to April – **Willow Warbler, Blackcap** and **Tree Pipit** may also be moving about in search of insects.

Look up and watch for the movements of **White-tailed Crested** and **African Dusky flycatchers**, which swoop out suddenly from the understorey and then return to their perches. You might see tiny 'winged boomerangs' heading your way – a **Scarce Swift** or **Black Saw-wing** – while in the skies above you, you may glimpse **African Crowned Eagle, Ayres's Hawk-Eagle, Mountain Buzzard** or **Great Sparrowhawk**.

All the while, the stunning **Bar-tailed Trogon** may be quietly perched on a high branch.

Black-fronted Bushshrike and **White-starred Robin** are harder to find, as are **Barred Long-tailed Cuckoo** and greenbuls (**Mountain, Yellow-whiskered** and **Slender-billed**), though their calls liven up the forest.

Fruiting trees attract hornbills (including **Crowned** and **Silvery-cheeked**), pigeons (**African Olive, Eastern Bronze-naped** and **African Green**), **Red-fronted Parrot, Hartlaub's Turaco** and **Sharpe's Starling**.

The narrow path leading down to the river starts behind the Gatamaiyu Fishing Camp site, where **African Black Duck** may be swimming under the cover of tree ferns and **Grey** and **Mountain wagtails** dart around. A second path on the left, about 1 km along the main track, takes you down a very steep and often slippery slope to a spectacular waterfall. However, the path is neither signposted nor easy to find.

OTHER WILDLIFE

Various animals, including elephant (usually in evidence from their dung piles) and the beautiful black-and-white colobus monkey occur here. A large variety of colourful forest butterflies can also be seen. The Gatamaiyu River is well known for trout fishing, but there are no river paths, and it is not easy to make a catch. (Wild rainbow trout are found in the pools upstream.) Otter families can occasionally be seen.

KINANGOP PLATEAU IBA

KEY SPECIES
Augur Buzzard, Grey Crowned Crane, Black-winged Plover, Nyanza Swift, Levaillant's Cisticola, Stout Cisticola, Long-tailed Widowbird, Jackson's Widowbird, Golden-winged Sunbird, Sharpe's Longclaw (E).

The Kinangop Plateau (2,377–2,440m) rises abruptly from the floor of the Rift Valley. The flat, raised plains extend for miles as far as the southern Aberdares in the east. The original tussock grasses and swamps that clothed these plains have been greatly reduced by farming, but the landscape still supports a variety of bird species not easily seen elsewhere. The most sought-after of these are **Long-tailed Widowbird**, **Jackson's Widowbird** and the Kenyan endemic **Sharpe's Longclaw**.

HABITAT
The plains are farmed intensively, with dairy cattle and sheep, wheat and other crops. Eucalyptus and cypress are grown on farm woodlots. A number of streams and rivers descend the steep gorges and drain into the Malewa River. Remnant forest patches occur on the western slopes of the plateau.

GETTING THERE
From Nairobi take the uplands road to Naivasha and Nakuru (A104). As you approach the left turn into Naivasha town, look out for a Total fuel station on your right. Turn right, straight after the Total, onto the road for North Kinangop and the Aberdare National Park. Drive up the escarpment, crossing the Karati River, and continuing until the tarmac ends (at Kirima Centre), and carry on along the murram road. The road to Sharpe's Longclaw Nature Reserve is signposted to the left at Murungaru town (there is also a sign for Aberdare National Park). Travel slowly for 4km on the corrugated road, then, where the track splits, keep right and you will pass some greenhousing (on your left). From this point, carry on for another 3km.

VISITOR INFO
All the land is privately owned, so most birding takes place from the roadside. On the northern end of the plateau, though, Nature Kenya has purchased a number of land parcels, one of which is Sharpe's Longclaw Nature Reserve in Murungaru. This is managed by Nature Kenya with the local group Friends of Kinangop Plateau (www.facebook.com/friendsofkinangopplateau), who are also able to provide a guide. There are three bandas for overnight accommodation at the reserve, and camping is also possible. There are other local options including Plovers Eco Camp (email: ruhiaa@gmail.com) and the Trees Guest House (naturekenya.org).

Jackson's Widowbird

THE BIRDING

It is not always easy to find the Kenyan endemic **Sharpe's Longclaw**, but it may be seen in grass fields by the road and, surprisingly, even in fields bustling with farming activity. Two pairs have bred at the Sharpe's Longclaw Nature Reserve.

Other species seen from a walk on the roads or in the reserve include **Cape Rook, Rufous-naped** and **Red-capped larks, Capped**

Jacques Pitteloud

Sharpe's Longclaw

Wheatear and **Golden-winged Sunbird.** You may be fortunate enough to chance upon the resplendent **Long-tailed Widowbird**, which has an extraordinarily long tail and red 'shoulders', or on **Jackson's Widowbird** leaping and calling in a spot chosen for courtship display.

Hunter's, the bright **Levaillant's** and brightly capped **Stout cisticolas** call attention to themselves with their calls. A walk in grassy fields can flush **Common Quail** and **Grass Owl**. In very wet conditions **African Snipe** breed here and can be found in display flight, their tail feathers drumming. **Common Stonechat** and, from October to April, **Pied Wheatear** are often perched on fence posts.

The grazed fields also attract **Grey Crowned Crane, Black-winged Plover, Mottled** and **Nyanza swifts, Red-throated Wryneck, Northern Anteater Chat, Yellow Bishop, Yellow Wagtail** (in season), **Yellow-throated Longclaw** and **Grassland Pipit.**

A variety of raptors can usually be seen flying over these grasslands, the most common of which is **Augur Buzzard.** On passage, all three migrant harriers (**Western Marsh, Pallid** and **Montagu's**) are seen here, as are **Lesser Kestrel, Eurasian Hobby** and **Common Buzzard.**

OTHER WILDLIFE

A highland endemic snake, the Kenya horned viper, and two endemic frogs are found on the Kinangop Plateau and are reliant upon the upland grasslands and wetlands to survive. Colobus monkey, scrub hare, tree hyrax and duiker are also occasionally seen.

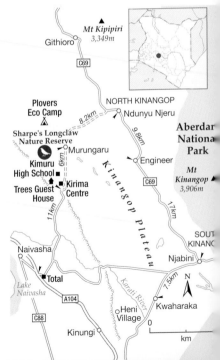

ABERDARE NATIONAL PARK IBA

KEY SPECIES
Jackson's Francolin, Aberdare Cisticola, Moorland Chat, Tacazze Sunbird, Scarlet-tufted Sunbird.

A volcanic range, the Aberdares extend north–south for almost 100km, are 40km across at their widest point, and form Kenya's most important water-catchment area. A 34km saddle of open tussock moorland, lying at an altitude of over 3,000m, separates the two highest peaks, Sattima (4,000m) in the north and Kinangop (3,906m) in the south. Here, and in the steep forested ravines cut by the range's many rivers, live a rich variety of highland birds including the Kenyan endemic **Aberdare Cisticola**.

HABITAT
The flora changes with altitude. As you drive up from the Kinangop Plateau you pass through montane forest with trees such as camphor *Ocotea usambarensis* and woodland waterberry *Syzygium guineense*, African pencil cedar *Juniperus procera*, a large belt of bamboo, and eventually, at even greater altitude, subalpine tree heath *Erica arborea* and hagenia *Hagenia abyssinica*. The beautiful moorlands occasionally give way to clear streams and amazing waterfalls.

GETTING THERE
If you are birding in North Kinangop, follow the directions to Kinangop (Site 8) to where the tarmac ends on the escarpment at Kirima Centre. Take a left turn at the signpost for Aberdare National Park. Drive 5km and pass Murungaru town, then keep right where the road forks. Stay on this road for about 8km, then turn right at the T-junction onto a tarred road. Continue for 2km and turn left, back onto a murram road

at the signpost for the park. Proceed through Ndunyu Njeru for 9km, passing the Outdoor Africa camp site on your right. Thereafter the road bends right for about 200m before it hits dilapidated tarmac again. The last 1.5km is an ascent that takes you through a corridor of electric wildlife fences to the park gate. On this stretch of the road there is a bridge where **Olive Ibis** have been seen. This

Peter Steward

Jackson's Francolin

road also goes through the bamboo belt – good habitat for **Abyssinian** and **Olive ground thrushes**.

From Nairobi, you may prefer to use the road via Njabini in South Kinangop. Take the Nairobi–Naivasha highway (A104) for about 65km to pass the centre of Soko Mjinga and go under the last flyover, 2.5km after the centre of Soko Mjinga. Soon after the flyover, exit the highway on the left to go around and pass over the highway towards the town of Flyover. Going straight on this road would get you to Thika, but instead you will continue for 1km and after a few bumps will turn left at the junction signposted for the towns of Magumu and Njabini. Continue for 22km to Njabini and turn left just before the Total Petrol Station in the direction of Engineer town (signposted 'Aberdare National Park').

THE BIRDING

Approaching the park's Matubio West Gate, especially in the chill early mornings just as the mist is lifting, you will come across numerous coveys of **Jackson's Francolin** out foraging on and beside the road. Also on the ascent to the park, look out for stunning long-tailed upland sunbirds (**Tacazze, Malachite** and **Golden-winged**) along with **Northern** and **Eastern double-collared sunbirds. Mountain Yellow** and **Brown Woodland warblers** are common here, as are **Yellow-bellied** and **Kandt's waxbills**. You may catch sight of an **African Crowned Eagle** displaying in the skies above.

On entering the park, look in the tussock moorland close to the gate for the endangered **Aberdare Cisticola**, which is common throughout this section of the park. **Moorland Chat**, confiding birds, whose white outer-tail feathers are strikingly apparent in flight, are also plentiful here, whether flying low over the road or perched atop clumps of giant heather on the roadside.

As the road descends gradually into the range's central saddle area, you may see **Scarlet-tufted Sunbird** flitting busily about in scenic meadows where red hot poker *Kniphofia* and everlasting flowers *Helichrysum* grow in the boggy ground.

Stop at any of the clear moorland streams and you might just glimpse **African Black** and **Yellow-billed ducks** or that most secretive

In highland forests listen for the flute-like call of the African Hill Babbler.

Jacques Pitteloud

Stay on the road to Engineer town, bearing left at a fork after 33km. At Engineer town turn right at the only T-junction. Continue for 7km, looking out for the National Oil Petrol Station on your left, and thereafter turn right to head through Ndunyu Njeru town, on a murram road that passes the Outdoor Africa camp site. From here, follow the directions as given on p.37.

follow the directions as given on p.37.

VISITOR INFO

You can access the park by paying the entry fee and showing identification. Camping is possible, but at these cooler altitudes, and with lots of buffalo about, you may prefer the self-catering houses. The Ark (www. thearkkenya.com) and Treetop Lodge (http://treetops.co.ke), both located in the east, in an area known as the Salient, are a luxurious option. Note that going off the main tracks requires a four-wheel drive.

of birds, the **African Finfoot**, swimming by. The melanistic (dark) morph of **Augur Buzzard** is especially common here, seen circling overhead or perched on distant *Hagenia* trees. **Mountain Buzzard** is another high-flying raptor to look out for.

After crossing the moorlands, there is a choice of roads descending the steep, wooded valleys of the range's eastern slopes to the gates leading out, one to the town of Nyeri and the other to Mweiga. Montane forest birds to look for on this descent include **African Emerald Cuckoo**, the **Black-fronted** and stunning **Doherty's bushshrikes, African Hill Babbler, Slender-billed, Waller's** and **Sharpe's starlings** and pairs of **Brown-capped Weaver**. Duetting pairs of **Hunter's Cisticola**, often seen singing from roadside perches, are always a particular treat, here and elsewhere in Kenya's moist central highlands.

OTHER WILDLIFE

Though they may be difficult to find, giant forest hog, side-striped jackal, melanistic serval (on the moorlands), golden cat, bongo, mountain bushbuck and endemic frogs and reptiles are all found in the Aberdares.

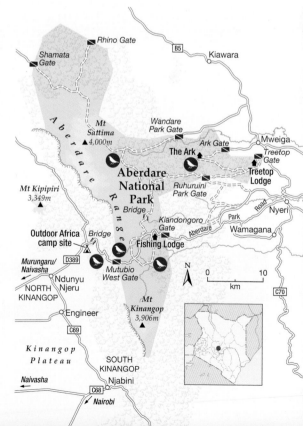

WAJEE NATURE PARK

KEY SPECIES
Hinde's Babbler, African Wood Owl.

This small, nearly 8ha park, set at an altitude of 1,620–1,700m in the highlands of central Kenya, was once a coffee farm, but has seen many years of tree planting and regeneration efforts and a woodland now covers the hillside. The park extends into a valley, where the endangered Kenyan endemic **Hinde's Babbler** can be found, both inside and outside the property.

HABITAT

Wajee is a green oasis in Mukurweini, an agricultural area where maize, beans, potatoes, horticultural crops, tea, coffee and livestock are farmed. Such extensive agriculture has resulted in the loss of much of the original habitat favoured by **Hinde's Babbler**, now increasingly confined to the thicket cover provided by the alien invasive *Lantana camara*, which colonizes valleys in Mukurweini that are not under cultivation.

GETTING THERE

Take Thika Highway (A2) from Nairobi and drive to the town of Karatina.

Continue along the A2 for 2km, then drive a further 2km from the town centre and take the Othaya–Karatina Road to your left. This beautiful winding road descends to cross the upper reaches of the Sagana River, before climbing again to reach the town of Mukurweini after about 13km. About 100m beyond the Mukurweini Law Courts the road forks – take the Mihuti Gakonya Road to your left and stay on it for 5km, looking out for the signpost to Wajee Nature Park on your left.

VISITOR INFO

This family-owned park receives visitors throughout the year. Wajee has a long trail, with two shorter trails connected to it. For a modest entry fee, you can walk along these trails, but be sure to consult a map before setting out.

You can book (**wajeenaturepark.co.ke**) traditional-style rondavels or rooms and a self-catering kitchen is available. A neighbouring restaurant is also starting up.

This woodland path lies in the valley at the Wajee Nature Park.

Wajee is home to the rare Hinde's Babbler.

THE BIRDING

Wajee is one of the best places in the country to see **Hinde's Babbler** – found in groups of a few individuals on the longer trail throughout the year. The trail starts behind the accommodation rooms, descends steeply through the woodland, and comes full circle along the valley where the property ends and ascends again. Look for the babblers in the *Lantana* on the other side of the low wire fence. They are very noisy, then go silent for a while before starting up again.

Other interesting highland species found in the park are **African Goshawk, Ayres's Hawk Eagle, Red-chested Cuckoo, Narina Trogon, Cinnamon-chested Bee-eater, Brown-hooded Kingfisher, Sulphur-breasted Bushshrike, Cinnamon Bracken Warbler, Montane White-eye, Rüppell's Robin Chat** and **Green-headed** and **Eastern Double-collared sunbirds. Trumpeter** and **Silvery-cheeked hornbills** and **Violet-backed Starling** stop here infrequently. **Verreaux's Eagle Owl** is also an irregular visitor but **African Wood Owl** can be found, often in the trees around the point where the trail is signposted '5'.

OTHER WILDLIFE

Because this is an intensively farmed region there are few animals: duiker tend to hide and are seldom seen, and genet, civet and bushbabies are active only at night.

Jacques Pitteloud

Hinde's Babbler

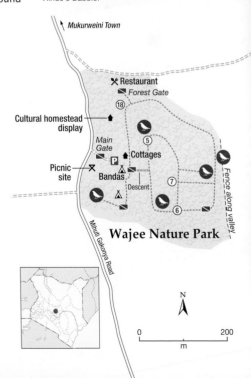

Mukurweini Town

Restaurant
Forest Gate
18
Cultural homestead display
Main Gate
5
Cottages
Picnic site
Bandas
Descent
7
6
Fence along valley

Wajee Nature Park

Mihuti Gakonya Road

N

0   200
m

SOUTH AND WEST MOUNT KENYA IBA

KEY SPECIES
Jackson's Francolin, African Black Duck, Olive Ibis, Mountain Buzzard, Mosque Swallow, Hunter's Cisticola, Abbott's Starling, Abyssinian Ground Thrush.

When the clouds roll back, beautiful Mount Kenya dominates the sky in the central highlands. The Kamweti Route is on the southern side of this extinct volcano and is seldom used for summiting the mountain. However, its lower reaches, covered with dense evergreen forest, are a great place for spotting highland and montane birds. It is best to request a guide and to be cautious while walking, owing to the numbers of elephant and bufflalo. On the more popular Naro Moru Route to the west, look out for birds as you drive to the Naro Moru Gate and around to the Meteorology ('Met') Station (3,048m) where the road ends.

HABITAT
The grassy track of the Kamweti Route traverses montane forest with trees such as camphor *Ocotea usambarensis* and African pencil cedar *Juniperus procera*. There is an open grassy glade at 2,055m, where Castle Forest Lodge is situated, and from here

The lower slopes of the mountain are covered with dense evergreen forest.

the bamboo zone is clearly visible above you. Beyond the lodge, the trail takes you past an old plantation before descending to the fern-lined Nyamindi River. The western, Naro Moru, route ascends more than 1,000m from Naro Moru town, passing farms, montane forest and bamboo.

GETTING THERE
Kamweti Route: From Nairobi take Thika Highway (the A2) past the towns of Thika, Kambiti, Kenol and Makuyu. When you reach Makutano, take the B6 east, passing the paddy fields and Wang'uru. After about 29km, turn left at 'Samson Corner', onto the C73 for Kutus. About 4.5km before Kutus there is a prominent turning to your right. Take this road and travel for about 2.5km until you reach a forked junction. Keep left and go past Kabare Girls' School for 6km until you reach a second fork. Keep to the left, heading in a northerly direction. You will pass Mutige Boys' Secondary School, Gatugura, some tea farms, Kimunye (and its tea factory) and a Kenyan 'tea zone' before reaching the edge of the forest on the slopes of Mount Kenya. Continue until you reach the gate of Castle Forest Station. (The distance from the prominent turn-off before Kutus to this gate is 22km.)

Naro Moru Route: From the A2 at Naro Moru take the road to the west of the mountain, which is signposted for Mount Kenya National Park. After 6km, look out for a sign indicating a road heading east to the Mount Kenya National Park Naro Moru Gate, which is 9.7km further on. The drive up to the Met Station from the gate is another 9.5km.

VISITOR INFO

Castle Forest Station Gate is open daily, and currently no entry fees are levied. In the west, on the Naro Moru Route, fees are due to the Kenya Wildlife Service. At Castle Forest Lodge (www.castleforestlodge.com) you can book rooms in the main house (built in 1910) or stay in a cottage, bungalow or at the camp site.

On the Naro Moru Route, the red soil road can be slippery when wet, so a four-wheel drive is advisable.

THE BIRDING

About a kilometre after the Castle Forest Station Gate and 2km before you reach Castle Forest Lodge there is a small bridge over the Thiba River. A weir on this river creates a pond. As you cross it you may spot **African Black Duck**. Here, too, the rare **Olive Ibis** has been observed, rather uncharacteristically out in the open at midmorning.

In the crisp mountain air the duet of **Hunter's Cisticola** seems especially shrill, the scarlet wings of **Hartlaub's Turaco** particularly vivid as it moves between trees, and the repeated honking of **Silvery-Cheeked Hornbill** much louder than usual.

Black-throated, Chestnut-throated and **Grey apalises**, **Montane White-eye**, **Tacazze, Northern** and **Eastern Double-collared sunbirds** and **Yellow-crowned Canary** are common in the few cedar trees and hedge bushes at Castle. Harder to observe, but still typical, are **Mountain, Yellow-whiskered** and **Slender-billed greenbuls**.

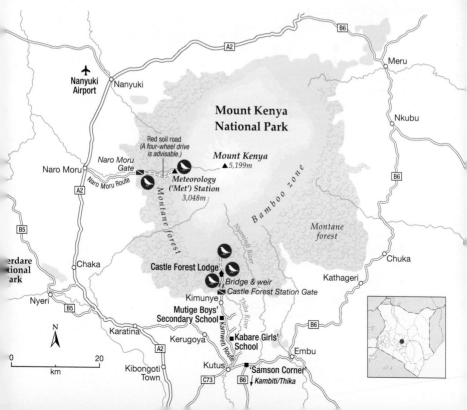

Jacques Pitteloud

Peter Steward

Black-fronted Bushshrike   Grey-headed Negrofinch

The forest closes in on the track after Castle Forest Lodge. It is a pleasant walk that may, in addition to greenbuls and starlings, turn up **African Olive Pigeon, Red-headed Parrot, Narina Trogon** and warblers – **Mountain Yellow** and **Brown Woodland warblers** and in season (October–April) **Willow** and **Garden warblers** and **Blackcap**. Other notable birds that you may encounter include **Black-fronted Bushshrike, African Hill Babbler, White-starred Robin, Grey-headed Negrofinch, Thick-billed Seedeater** and **Oriole Finch**.

Back at the lodge, check the area around the swimming pool (where elephant often come to drink). You'll find **Common, Black-crowned** and numerous **Yellow-bellied waxbills** in the grass nearby, while overhead you may see **White-headed** and **Black saw-wings, Mosque Swallow** and, in season, **Barn Swallow. Mountain Buzzard, African Harrier Hawk** and **Rufous-breasted Sparrowhawk** also scout from the skies above for rodents and hyrax.

Mount Kenya is a refuge for the threatened **Abbott's Starling** and it, together with **Olive Ibis**, is a special sighting. Both species occasionally stop in the grounds of Castle Forest Lodge. Look out for the ibis at dusk.

On your way to visit the Meteorology ('Met') Station (3,048m) on the more popular Naro Moru Route on the west side of the mountain, keep a lookout for **White-headed Wood-hoopoe** and **Cinnamon Bracken Warbler**. Birders come up this way especially for **Abyssinian Ground Thrush** and **Jackson's Francolin**, which occur among the timberline vegetation of the Met Station. **Scarlet-tufted Malachite Sunbirds** feed on *Lobelia telekii* flowers on the moorlands – reached only after at least two days of mountain climbing. This sunbird and **Moorland Chat** are easier to see in the Aberdares (Site 9).

OTHER WILDLIFE

Except for the familiar barking of colobus monkeys, the animals in the forest are not always obvious, but they include buffalo, leopard, hyena, hyrax and porcupine, as well as herds of elephant that come and go. The bongo is also seen, but is rare.

LAIKIPIA

KEY SPECIES
Stone Partridge, Verreaux's Eagle, Great Spotted Cuckoo, Marsh Owl, White-headed Mousebird, Bearded Woodpecker, Red-throated Wryneck, Grey-headed Bushshrike, Taita Fiscal, Magpie Starling. **Passage migrants:** Madagascar Pond Heron (Malagasy migrant), Lesser Kestrel, Eurasian Wryneck.

Laikipia is a vast semi-arid region covering 9,720km² in central Kenya. Here, pastoralists and large commercial ranchers drive cattle, although the region also includes some forest reserves and agricultural areas. Laikipia is known for its inselbergs, the Milima Tatu and Mukenya peaks, the Lolldaiga Hills in the near northeast, and Mount Kenya filling the far eastern horizon, so the views in this region are sensational. The birds found here are generally typical of dry acacia bush and grassland, with some variation, depending on how far north or south you are birding.

HABITAT
Much of Laikipia sits on a plateau at a height of between 1,600 and 1,800m. Most of it is bushland, interrupted by escarpments and flat areas of grass. Thorn trees dominate the landscape, which tends to be a uniform grey-brown in the dry months. *Acacia etbaica*, prickle thorn *Acacia brevispica* and black thorn *Acacia mellifera* are interspersed with the green tops of *Boscia* spp. and an understorey of orange-and-green-leafed croton *Croton dichogamus*. Flowering thorn trees and *Ipomoea* bushes provide occasional bursts of colour. Yellow fever trees *Acacia xanthophloea* flank the Ewaso Ny'iro and Ewaso Narok rivers and their seasonal tributaries, while whistling thorn *Acacia drepanolobium* and euclea *Euclea divinorum* are found where black cotton soil is prevalent. Biocontrol efforts are ongoing to stall the invasive *Opuntia* cactus, which is widespread in the area.

GETTING THERE
Starting from the Nakumatt supermarket building in Nanyuki, drive north on the A2 and turn left onto the Nanyuki–Rumuruti Road (C76). Drive for 8.7km and then turn right. For Lolldaiga Hills, turn right again after 6.5km. For Mpala, continue straight on for 33km – the first 13km are on tarmac, but thereafter the road is murram. Suyian is 50km beyond Mpala. For any destination that you plan to visit in Laikipia, make sure you first enquire for specific directions.

VISITOR INFO
Go to www.laikipiatourism.com to find places to stay. Camp sites, cottages and ranch houses are available in addition to camps and lodges. Parts of properties may not be open to the public throughout the year, and a conservancy fee may also be charged. Be mindful that ranches are large, the distances are vast and there is little signage.

Typical big skies and bush scenery along a track at Mpala in the dry season

THE BIRDING

■ *Along the Ewaso Ny'iro River:* Fever trees, scrub and the occasional fig tree along the Ewaso Ny'iro attract **Goliath Heron**, **Brown Parrot**, kingfishers, **Red-fronted Barbet**, **Scaly-throated Honeyguide**, **Bearded** and **African Grey woodpeckers** and the stunning **Grey-headed** and **Sulphur-breasted bushshrikes**. Feeding on the muddy edges of the river there may be **Black Crake** and in season (October–April) **Little Ringed Plover**, **Green** and **Wood sandpipers** and other waders. On an early morning visit, look for the reserved **African Finfoot** – and watch out for hippo, too!

■ *Acacia bush:* It is worth exploring the many kilometres of track that run through the thorn bush in Laikipia. **Great Spotted Cuckoo** may be calling from perches and, in northerly areas, flocks of the uncommon **White-headed Mousebird** may descend on a tree. **Abyssinian Scimitarbill**, **Rosy-patched Bushshrike**, **Pringle's Puffback**, **Northern White-crowned Shrike** and **Grey-headed and African silverbills** are other residents. Likely migrants (in season) include **Eurasian Wryneck**, **Eastern Olivaceous** and **Willow warblers** and **Isabelline** and **Northern wheatears**. Ground-feeding birds (**Shelley's**, **Crested** and **Hildebrandt's francolins**, **Lichtenstein's Sandgrouse** and families of guineafowl) are not difficult to find, despite the grass and low scrub.

In the more open grassland, with its scattered whistling thorn *Acacia drepanolobium* and euclea, you can expect a diversity of larks, bustards and coursers. Birds that may be easier to find here include **Jacobin Cuckoo**, **Rufous-crowned Roller**, **Taita Fiscal**, **Golden** (Afrotropic migrant) and **Plain-backed pipits** (in season), **Eurasian Bee-eater** and **Common Rock Thrush**. Raptors may include **Lesser Kestrel** (in season), **Bateleur** and **Montagu's** (in season) and **African Marsh** (uncommon) **harriers**. On the plains a good sign that a 'kill' has taken place is the gathering of vultures in a tree, usually consisting of **White-backed**, **Rüppell's** and **Lappet-faced vultures**.

Birds that come down from the more arid north and wanderers from the highlands that border Laikipia may surprise you – **Narina Trogon**, **Purple-throated Cuckooshrike** and **Grey-capped Warbler** have all been spotted.

■ *Mpala Research Centre:* Mpala (**mpala. org**), which lies in the centre of Laikipia County, welcomes students, educators and researchers and offers camping facilities for groups. The centre has an electric fence with a ring road inside it, so it is possible to walk around here. It is an excellent place to find the common birds of the semi-arid thorn bush.

Walking around the ring road may produce **Northern Grey Tit**, **Grey Wren Warbler**, **Yellow-bellied Eremomela**, **Red-faced Crombec**, **Banded Parisoma**, **Rufous Chatterer**, **Hunter's** and **Marico sunbirds**, **Vitelline Masked Weaver** and **Steel-blue Whydah**. From the ring road, take the short drive towards the camp

Vulturine Guineafowl with chicks

Dino Martins

site and midway along there is an active **Martial Eagle's** nest atop a fever tree on the left of the road. **Steppe** (in season) and **Verreaux's eagle**s are also seen.

■ *Along the Ewaso Narok River:* Seen near the more northern sections of the river is **Violet-backed Woodhoopoe** and flocks of **Magpie Starling, African Black Duck** in the rainy season or when the river is flowing, and **Striated Heron** and **Verreaux's Eagle Owl**.

Look out also for **Three-Streaked Tchagra, Mouse-coloured Penduline Tit, Fan-tailed Raven** and **Ethiopian Swallow**. Take a picnic lunch and you may see **Stone Partridge** stepping out from cover. Also seen on rock faces in Laikipia is **Mocking Cliff Chat**; while above high cliffs **Marsh Owl** hunt over areas of extensive grasslands in the early evening. (Situated north of the Ewaso Narok River is Suyian Ranch **www.suyian.com.** Check to see if it is possible to visit.)

Jacques Pitteloud

Ethiopian Swallow

■ *Lolldaiga Hills Farm House:* Situated in the eastern highland sector of Laikipia, this ranch (**www.lolldaiga.com**) lies at an elevation of about 1,700–2,300m. The vegetation here is remnant forest comprising 'podo' or Outeniqua yellowwood *Podocarpus falcatus*, African pencil cedar *Juniperus procera* and wild olive *Olea* spp. **Red-throated Wryneck** (after rains), **Boran Cisticola** and **Pale Flycatcher** are common here. A scattering of watering holes and dams for cattle attract ducks and waders and also bring in **African Spoonbill, Dwarf Bittern** and the endangered Malagasy migrant **Madagascar Pond Heron**.

OTHER WILDLIFE

Cheetah, wild dog and the 'big five' are found in Laikipia, as well as Günther's dik-dik, bush hyrax, dwarf mongoose, bush and striped squirrel. If you are driving at dusk, try not to run over Cape hare and shrews, which are often found on or alongside the road.

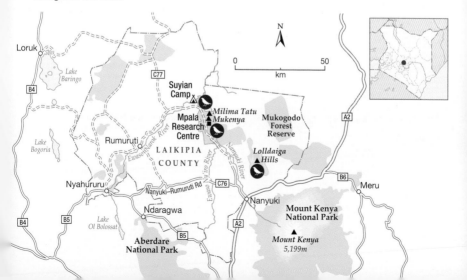

SITE 13

SAMBURU AND BUFFALO SPRINGS NATIONAL RESERVES **IBA**

KEY SPECIES
Pygmy Falcon, Peregrine Falcon, Shikra, Martial Eagle, Blue-naped Mousebird, Somali Bee-eater, Yellow-vented Eremomela, Somali Crombec, Donaldson Smith's Sparrow Weaver, Black-capped Social Weaver, Magpie Starling, Bristle-crowned Starling.

The Samburu and Buffalo Springs national reserves share a river boundary in a semi-desert area in north-central Kenya. The rains turn the dry, grey-brown land into a verdant wilderness, fill dry *luggas* and swell the Ewaso Ny'iro River. The river, with its riparian trees and surrounding protected habitat, provides a refuge, drawing wildlife and more than 400 bird species, including **Donaldson Smith's Sparrow Weaver**, **Magpie Starling** and **Bristle-crowned Starling**, which are otherwise common only in the arid north of the country.

HABITAT
These small reserves are set in beautiful territory in the lower limits of the northern rangelands. The habitat of Samburu (165km²) and Buffalo Springs (131km²) is semi-deciduous bushland with *Acacia tortilis* and *Commiphora*, scattered flowering aloes and desert rose *Adenium obesum*. The Ewaso Ny'iro and its tributaries are dominated by *Acacia elatior* (or *eldebess*), fork-trunked doum palm *Hyphaene compressa* and tamarind (*msisi*) and is one of three places in the country where you find the Tana River poplar *Populus ilicifolia*. Inselbergs dot the landscape, the most conspicuous of which is Koitigor Hill.

GETTING THERE
Coming from Nairobi on the A2 you will pass to the west of Mount Kenya. As you travel northwards, you will see wheat and canola fields on the lower slopes of the mountain and get your first glimpse of the endless miles of plains, hills, inselbergs and mountain ranges that characterize the northern country. After Timau, the road begins a 600m descent down the escarpment to Isiolo. (**Rattling** and **Boran cisticolas** are present on this stretch.) From here, it is a 38km journey via the town of Archer's Post to reach the Samburu National Reserve's Archer's Post Gate. Between Isiolo and Archer's Post there are two turn-offs to the left (at 20km and 31km) to Buffalo Springs.

VISITOR INFO
The reserves are open year-round and are managed by Isiolo County. The entry fee gives you access to both reserves as well as to Shaba, which is due east, on the other side of the A2. The heavy rains in March and April bring the land to life, but may cause flash floods. When the Ewaso Ny'iro River fills it sometimes sweeps away the bridge that connects Samburu National Reserve in the north with Buffalo Springs National Reserve in the south.

The dramatic cliff faces of Ol Donyo Sabache (to the right), as seen from Buffalo Springs

Peter Usher

THE BIRDING

■ *Lodges and camps:* The gardens of
many lodges and camps in the area have
a rich variety of species, including the
Spotted Palm Thrush, whose sweet
song announces the dawn at many sites,
Abyssinian Scimitarbill, **Black-throated
Barbet**, **Black-bellied** and (uncommon)
Shining sunbirds, **Bare-eyed Thrush**,
White-headed Buffalo Weaver and **White-
bellied Canary**. Rushing about in search
of flying insects there may be **Mottled
Swift**, **Wire-tailed**, **Lesser Striped** and
Red-rumped swallows and **Rock Martin**.

African Orange-bellied Parrot

■ *Riverine forest:* The riparian woods
may hold **African Orange-bellied Parrot**,
Lesser and Scaly-throated honeyguides,
Sulphur-breasted Bushshrike and colonies of **Lesser Masked** and **Golden Palm**
weavers. **Verreaux's Eagle Owl** is conspicuous by day, while at dusk you are likely
to hear the siren-like call of **Slender-tailed Nightjar**.

■ *Ewaso Ny'iro River:* The river lures elephant herds to drink, but also brings
herons and egrets, **African Spoonbill**, **Water Thick-knee** and **Malachite
Kingfisher**. When the river is low, sand bars appear and are frequented by
crocodile and hippo and by waders like **Spur-winged**, **Little Ringed** and **Three-
banded plovers** and **Green** and **Wood sandpipers**.

■ *Bushland:* As you drive along, look on or beside the tracks for **Vulturine
Guineafowl** and **Crested Francolin**. Other notable birds to watch for are **Blue-
naped Mousebird**, **Somali Bee-eater**, **Eastern Yellow-billed Hornbill**, **Fan-tailed
Raven**, **Yellow-vented Eremomela**, **Somali Crombec** and starlings (**Golden-
breasted**, **Fischer's**, **Magpie** and **Bristle-crowned**).

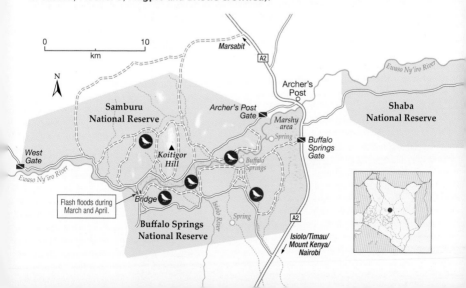

Grasshopper Buzzard

Both reserves can be good for raptors – look for **Pygmy Falcon** (which take over the nests of **White-headed Buffalo-Weavers**), **African Black-shouldered Kite**, **Pallid Harrier** (in season), **Shikra**, **African Hawk Eagle** and the endangered **Egyptian** and **Lappet-faced** and critically endangered **Hooded, Rüppell's** and **White-headed vultures**. You may also see – often perched in trees – **Peregrine Falcon, Gabar Goshawk, Grasshopper Buzzard** (an Afrotropic migrant, November–March) and **Martial Eagle**. In season (October–March) there may be flocks of **Lesser Kestrel, Sooty Falcon** and **Common Buzzard**.

Whydahs (**Pin-tailed, Eastern Paradise, Steel-blue** and **Straw-tailed**) are also seen in this open bushland.

■ *Buffalo Springs National Reserve:* This reserve is named for the clear springs situated near its eastern border. They are surrounded by low walls, which create small reservoirs (one of which captures water for the town of Archer's Post). Some seepage still occurs nearby, and the resulting marshy area attracts **Reed Cormorant, African Darter** and **Black Crake**. **Yellow Wagtail** may also be present in season.

A drive around the sparsely vegetated southern plains can turn up **Abyssinian Scimitarbill, Fawn-coloured Lark, Chestnut-headed** and **Fischer's sparrow larks**, nesting **Donaldson Smith's Sparrow Weaver, Black-capped Social Weaver** and **Grey-headed** (Parrot-billed) and **Chestnut sparrows**.

OTHER WILDLIFE

Of special note are those animals found in northern Kenya that survive in arid conditions with very little water, including Grevy's zebra, reticulated giraffe, gerenuk and the beisa oryx.

Donaldson Smith's Sparrow Weaver

SHABA NATIONAL RESERVE IBA

KEY SPECIES

African Swallow-tailed Kite, White-headed Mousebird, Williams's Lark (E), Red-winged Lark, Pink-breasted Lark, Chestnut-headed Sparrow Lark, Yellow-billed Oxpecker, Brown-tailed Rock Chat, Fire-fronted Bishop. **Passage migrants:** Blue-cheeked Bee-eater, Red-backed Shrike, Lesser Grey Shrike.

The Ewaso Ny'iro River forms the northern border of the lovely Shaba National Reserve, which measures about 239km² in area. The grass and scrub here are normally golden brown, but after the rains the reserve explodes with colourful flowers, and the open woodlands are decked out in shades of green and grey. This is the preferred habitat of the Kenyan endemic **Williams's Lark**.

HABITAT

At Shaba, doum palms *Hyphaene compressa* grow along the river, and there are stretches of umbrella thorn *Acacia tortilis* woodland and rocky grassland, as well as lava outcrops and saltwater springs and swamps. On opposite sides of the reserve lie Mount Bodech in the north and Mount Shaba in the south, while even further north, the majestic flat-topped Ol Donyo Sabache dominates the volcanic landscape of north-central Kenya.

GETTING THERE

From the town of Isiolo (see directions for Site 13) it is 33km to the turn-off for Shaba National Reserve and a further 5km drive to the reserve's Natorbi Ogura Gate.

VISITOR INFO

Shaba National Reserve is managed by Isiolo County. The daily entry fee gives you access both to Shaba and to the Samburu and Buffalo Springs national reserves. Ask at the gate for the latest advice on security. There are few places to stay, but Sarova Shaba Game Lodge (www.sarovahotels.com/shabalodge-samburu/) on the Ewaso Ny'iro River is a popular option.

The winding Ewaso Ny'iro River with the hills of the northern rangelands in the distance

THE BIRDING

Although the environment seems hotter here, the bird species found are similar to those in the Samburu and Buffalo Springs national reserves located 9km to the west (see Site 13).

Rosy-patched Bushshrikes duetting

Check the rocky lava plains close to the main gate for **Brown-tailed Rock Chat**. Take the track east from the Sarova Shaba Game Lodge, which splits after about 2km, with the left-hand track passing close to the river. Continuing straight on, the grassland is dotted with thorn trees and becomes very scrubby in places. You may see **White-headed** and **Blue-naped mousebirds** clinging to the tops of the trees, gorgeous **Red-and-yellow Barbet** foraging for insects, pairs of **Rosy-patched Bushshrike** calling in courtship display, and **Golden Pipit** (an Afrotropic migrant) in flight. In season (October–April) look for **Red-backed** and **Lesser Grey shrikes**, **Marsh**, **Eastern Olivaceous** and **Barred warblers**, **Rufous Bush Chat** and wheatears.

Continue on this track for a few kilometres, looking out for more rocky lava plains, and check amid the grass stubble for the very localized **Williams's Lark**. Although the literature on Shaba often mentions **Masked Lark**, another special of the area, it is actually rare here. You'd do better to explore areas further east (requiring extra security) or the desert country north of Marsabit. However, resident larks include **Chestnut-headed Sparrow Lark** and the **Red-winged**, **Foxy**, **Pink-breasted** and **Fawn-coloured larks**, their song a constant accompaniment on any drive.

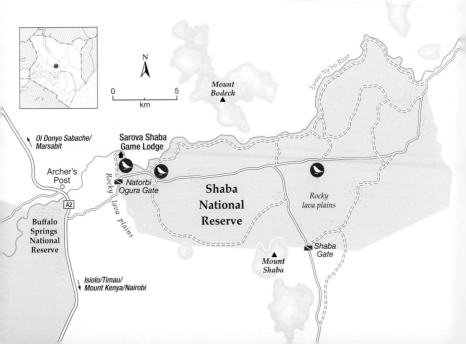

Other notable birds to expect at Shaba are **Pringle's Puffback, Taita Fiscal, Northern Grey Tit, Mouse-coloured Penduline Tit**, the **Ashy, Tiny** and **Desert cisticolas, Somali Crombec** (uncommon), **Banded Parisoma**, bustards (including **Heuglin's Bustard**) and a variety of birds of prey, similar to those seen at Site 13. Also look out for **African Swallow-tailed Kite**. Well camouflaged against the stubbly, rocky ground may be **Spotted Thick-knee, Temminck's** and **Somali coursers** and **Chestnut-bellied** and **Lichtenstein's sandgrouse**.

White-throated Bee-eaters

Somali, White-throated (Afrotropic migrant) and, in season, **Blue-cheeked bee-eaters** are also commonly seen. Riding the backs of reticulated giraffe you may spot **Yellow-billed Oxpecker**, while **Somali Ostrich** may be keeping their distance in the background. In the rainy season keep a lookout at wetlands, such as the one near to the Sarova Shaba Game Lodge, for breeding pairs of **Fire-fronted Bishop**, with their puffy yellow backs and bright red head patches.

OTHER WILDLIFE

The wildlife mentioned under Samburu and Buffalo Springs national reserves (see Site 13) is also found at Shaba. African savanna hare, striped hyena, the rare aardwolf and waterbuck are other species that occur in these northern reserves.

The Somali Ostrich is a subspecies of the Common Ostrich.

LAKE TURKANA [IBA]

KEY SPECIES
Greater Flamingo, Pink-backed Pelican, Heuglin's Bustard, Spur-winged Plover, Kittlitz's Plover, African Skimmer, Abyssinian Roller, Northern Carmine Bee-eater, Abyssinian Ground Hornbill, Crested Lark, Thekla Lark, Magpie Starling, Brown-tailed Rock Chat. **Passage migrants:** Common Ringed Plover, Caspian Plover, Little Stint.

Turkana is a massive lake in the middle of a hot, dry desert landscape that is both forbidding and incredibly beautiful. It is located just south of Kenya's border with South Sudan and Ethiopia and has three fascinating islands: North, Central and South islands. North Island is closest to Sibiloi National Park on Turkana's eastern shores. Central Island National Park is halfway down the lake, while South Island National Park lies at the lake's southern end. Large numbers of resident water birds occur on Lake Turkana, including **African Skimmer**. It is also a major wintering ground for **Little Stint** and an important passage site for migrants on their northward migration (March–April).

African Skimmer feeding

HABITAT
Turkana is often called the 'jade sea', owing to its turquoise colour. The water is brackish, but is just drinkable. Its shoreline is about 600km long, and its surface area is around 6,750 km². The water level fluctuates by 1–1.5m at a time and is expected to drop considerably with the completion of a dam on the Omo River in Ethiopia. It is fringed in places by *Typha* bulrushes and *Potomageton* pondweed, which provide important spawning grounds for fish that feed on phytoplankton. These fish, in turn, support diverse birdlife. The swamp vegetation in the deltas of the Omo, Turkwel and Kerio rivers, which feed the lake, is increasingly being smothered by invasive species, including the thorny shrub *Prosopis* and water hyacinth *Eichhornia crassipes*.

The vegetation on the eastern side of the lake is a mix of scrubby *Acacia-Commiphora* bushland and open semi-desert with dwarf *Indigofera spinosa,* which is heavily grazed upon by camels and goats. West and south of the lake, the dry seasonal sand *luggas* are fringed with *Acacia tortilis* and *A. elatior* woodlands (sometimes supported by ground water) and doum palms. The wild flowers here are spectacular after the rains, among them stands of radiant *Gloriosa minor* and fields of yellow *Tribulus terrestris*.

GETTING THERE
Most of the Turkana region is remote and rugged, and the distances are vast. The roads are dusty, sometimes obscure, made of sand or lava rock, and most lack signage.

Peter Usher

Wentai Tong

Grass homesteads in the vast landscape of Turkana

In addition, there are large sandy *luggas* to cross. Most people fly in: commercial airlines run daily flights to Lodwar, where many private vehicles are available for hire. (Four-wheel drive is essential.) Travelling overland from further south is a major undertaking, requiring extra fuel, water and, in some places, security.

VISITOR INFO

Climatic conditions can be challenging for visitors. Rainfall is typically erratic and unpredictable. Years can pass in total drought, but when rain does fall it can be torrential. Temperatures normally range between about 19°C and 39°C, with a mean daily temperature of around 29°C. In some areas the daytime temperatures can exceed 50°C, and soil surface temperatures of up to 70°C have been recorded.

On the western side of Lake Turkana, there are a number of places to stay. You can arrange to visit the Catholic mission of Todonyang (mcspa.org) to the far northwest of the lake, or you can camp at Eliye Springs Resort (www.eliyespringsresort.com) or Lobolo Camp (www.jadeseajourneys. com), both of which are on the lakeshore,

a couple of hours from Lodwar. Also to the west of Lake Turkana, the Turkana Basin Institute (www.turkanabasin.org) has a campus and accommodation for students and scientists at Nachekichok on the Turkwel River, about 30km east of Lodwar. The institute has another facility at Ileret, east of Lake Turkana and just south of the Kenyan–Ethiopian border.

Also on the eastern shore are the Koobi Fora bandas (book with the National Museums of Kenya, publicrelations@ museums.or.ke) and Alia Bay Guest House (reservations@kws.go.ke), which are self-catering. Both are in Sibiloi National Park, which protects major palaeontological, mammalian and other fossil finds, including a petrified forest.

To go bird-watching on the islands, contact a reputable company like Jade Sea Journeys (www.jadeseajourneys.com) to hire a boat that can handle the long distances and strong currents. If visiting South Island, pay the KWS fees at the Loiyangalani office. For Central Island, pay at the Kalakol KWS office or at Sibiloi's KWS offices at Alia Bay.

Abyssinian Roller

THE BIRDING

In almost any sheltered bay along the lakeshore you will see **Greater Flamingo**, **Yellow-billed Stork**, **Pink-backed Pelican**, **Reed Cormorant** and **Kittlitz's Plover**. In season (October–April) the many **Lesser Black-backed** and **Slender-billed** gulls and the **Gull-billed**, **Caspian** (uncommon), **Sandwich** (also uncommon) and **White-winged Black** terns lend the lake a seaside atmosphere.

From Lodwar, travel over the plains to Eliye Springs Resort or north to Kalakol, Ferguson's Gulf and beyond. The shoreline is variously sandy and rocky (and it's muddy at the river deltas) but you may be rewarded with **Western Reef Heron** (an Afrotropic migrant), **African Darter**, **African Fish Eagle**, **Greater Painted-snipe**, **Grey-headed Gull**, **African Skimmer** and **Dwarf** and **Fan-tailed ravens**. In season, **Osprey**, abundant **Spur-winged**, **Common Ringed** and **Caspian** plovers, **Black-tailed Godwit**,

SOUTH SUDAN

ETHIOPIA

Our Lady
Queen of Peace
Catholic Church
Todonyang
Ileret
Turkana Basin
Institute
C47 Lowarengak
Nariokotome
North
Island
Sibiloi
National
Park
Koobi Fora
Field School
Lomekwi
Kataboi
Alia
Bay
Alia Bay
Guest House

KENYA Ferguson's
Gulf
Kalakol
Central Island
National Park
Lobolo
Camp
Eliye Springs
Resort
Lodwar Turkwel River
A1
Turkana
Basin Institute
C77

N

0   10
km

Loiyangalan

South Island
National Park

Spotted Redshank, Little Stint, Curlew Sandpiper and Yellow Wagtail are also found along the shore. Working the lake and surrounding areas may be **Fox Kestrel** (uncommon), **Eastern Chanting Goshawk** and **African Hawk Eagle**. **Western Marsh** and **Montagu's harriers** can also occur in season.

The woodlands and bush along the Turkwel River are good places to find **White-bellied Go-away-bird**, **Abyssinian Roller**, **Northern Carmine Bee-eater** (Afrotropic migrant, November–February), **Somali Fiscal**, **Isabelline Shrike** (in season) and **Magpie** and **Bristle-crowned starlings**. **Red-billed**, **Eastern Yellow-billed** and **Jackson's hornbills** abound in more wooded areas with larger trees. Bush birds may be few but typically include **Meyer's Parrot**, **Abyssinian Scimitarbill**, **Red-and-yellow Barbet** and **Green-winged Pytilia**.

A drive or walk across the semi-desert landscape occasionally yields bustards (including the rare **Heuglin's Bustard**) and striking pairs of **Abyssinian Ground Hornbill**. Also often seen are **Pygmy Falcon**, **Senegal Thick-knee**, **Somali Courser**, **Crested** and **Thekla larks**, **Chestnut-headed Sparrow Lark** and **Red-throated Pipit** (in season).

Pygmy Falcon

Magpie Starling

One of the most magical experiences in Turkana is watching large flocks of sandgrouse coming to drink from the rivers or shallow bays, and then flying back out into the desert. The confiding **Brown-tailed Rock Chat**, which will approach closely at camps, is also charming.

OTHER WILDLIFE

Over 40 species of fish, including some endemics, occur here, and there is a thriving local fishery based mainly on Nile perch and Nile tilapia. Seasonally, wild flowers support a huge diversity of bees, including the recently described endemic *Samba turkana*. Thousands of Nile crocodiles nest on the lake's islands, although their numbers are declining, both because fishermen raid their nests and because an increase in the number of goats is threatening their habitat. Be wary of the numerous scorpions and snakes. Mosquitos may also be present in epic numbers.

SITE 16

MERU NATIONAL PARK IBA

KEY SPECIES

Saddle-billed Stork, Palm-nut Vulture, African Orange-bellied Parrot, Pel's Fishing Owl, Madagascar Bee-eater, Buff-bellied Warbler, Green-capped Eremomela, Hinde's Babbler (E), Black-bellied Sunbird. **Passage migrants:** Eurasian Roller, Blue-cheeked Bee-eater.

Located on the equator, Meru National Park slopes from an altitude of over 850m in the northwest down to 300m on its southeastern boundary at the Tana River, growing hotter and harsher along the way. The 870km² park is an interesting mix: it is mostly hot and dry, but has numerous watercourses, and it is in an area in which birds associated with more northerly, southerly and even coastal ranges overlap.

HABITAT

A number of streams arising from the Nyambene Hills run through the park, converge into a few larger rivers and join the Tana River along the park's southeastern boundary. *Acacia robusta* and *A. elatior,* figs, *Newtonia hildebrandtii* (known as *mukui*), raffia palms and the wild date palm *Phoenix reclinata* are seen on different stretches of the river. This is one of three places in the country where you will find the Tana River poplar *Populus ilicifolia.* Many seasonal marshes occur in the northwest of the park.

GETTING THERE

Travelling on the D484 road from Meru, turn left at the signpost for Meru National Park, about 3km before Maua, and continue for 26km to the Murera Gate. Beware of reckless drivers delivering 'miraa' (khat) to Nairobi!

If you have a four-wheel drive, an alternative is to take the B6 past Embu and turn right soon after Ena market onto the C92 at the signpost for Ura Gate. Continue along this scenic road to Ishiara and go 1.5km past the Total fuel station. Turn right

at the signs for Chiakariga schools, drive for about 3km, then turn left at the 'Ura Gate 52km' sign. The road is challenging for about 17km until you arrive at Marimanti, where you will join an all-weather road. Turn right and continue through the centres of Gaciongo and Gatunga to Ura Gate. (If the rough section of road is repaired this will be a more scenic route to the park.)

VISITOR INFO

Joy Adamson's book *Born Free* (1960), about Elsa the lioness, and the film that followed, made Meru the best-known park in Kenya. However, visitors abandoned it for decades, owing to heavy poaching. Happily, with the help of donors, including the International Fund for Animal Welfare and the French Agency for Development, it has recovered. Kenya Wildlife Service manages the park, and there are a number of camp sites and self-catering bandas (including Bwatherongi, which has a swimming pool). Note that tsetse fly may be a nuisance. Phone the tourism office at the park: +254 786 348 875 or email: **meru.tourism@gmail.com**.

Doum palms tower over the plains and open woodlands of Meru National Park.

THE BIRDING

■ *Plains and wetlands:* In the dry season the yellow grass of the hot plains south of the Murera Gate give way to large bare patches that offer good views of bustards, **Black-faced Sandgrouse** and the mounds that are the haunt of **Yellow-necked Spurfowl**. The grassland may have plenty of **Black-headed Plover**, with their distinct long thin crests, **Red-winged** and **Pink-breasted larks, Chestnut-backed Sparrow Lark, Chestnut-headed Sparrow Lark**, an uncommon northern species, and **Fischer's Sparrow Lark** (normally absent from the east and north of the country).

In season (October–April), you can't miss the migrants for sheer numbers: brilliant cyan **Eurasian Roller, Red-backed** and **Lesser Grey shrikes, Isabelline** and **Pied wheatears, Common Rock Thrush, Spotted Flycatcher** and numerous martins and swallows magnificently adorn the park. Both **Black-bellied** and **Hartlaub's bustards** also occur.

Raptors are another group of birds whose numbers are really impressive. Look for **Lanner** and **Taita falcons, African Cuckoo Hawk, African Black-shouldered Kite, Black-chested Snake Eagle, Bateleur** and **Grasshopper Buzzard** (Afrotropic migrant). In season, **Lesser Kestrel**, falcons and harriers, **Long-legged Buzzard** and **Steppe** and **Booted eagles** are common. The rare **African Swallow-tailed Kite** is also infrequently recorded.

African Finfoot likes to swim under the overhanging forest foliage along the upper reaches of the Bisanadi, Murera, Kindani, Rojewero and other rivers. In this vicinity **African Darter, African Orange-bellied Parrot, Verreaux's Eagle Owl, Red-fronted Tinkerbird** and **Golden Palm Weaver** are also likely. **Zanzibar** and **Yellow-bellied greenbuls** may be moving about in the low canopy, and the white form of the **African**

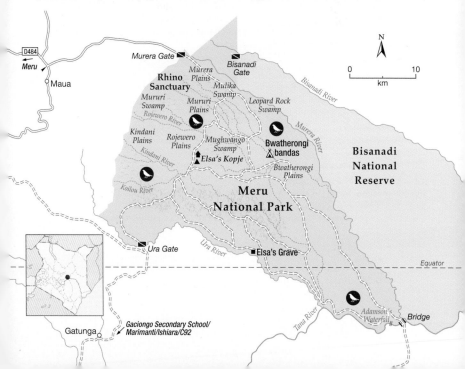

Black-bellied Sunbird

Paradise Flycatcher is also common. Look out for **Crested Guineafowl** (usually found on the coast and in highland forests) on the edge of the forest near the tracks.

Many of the camp sites and the few lodges are near rivers – look in the gardens and in the forest edging the river for **Trumpeter Hornbill**, **White-eared Barbet**, **Buff-bellied Warbler**, **Green-capped Eremomela**, **Red-capped Robin Chat**, **Southern Black** and **Pale flycatchers**, **Hunter's Sunbird**, the uncommon **Shining Sunbird** and the highly localized **Black-bellied Sunbird**.

In between the rivers in the northwest there are open woodlands that host a population of the Kenyan endemic **Hinde's Babbler** (found both inside and outside the park). Note that remnant forest patches north of the park are the most reliable locality for the rare **Black-and-white Flycatcher**.

The rivers form swamps, such as the Mururi, Bwatherongi and Mulika swamps located near the Murera Gate, which are popular with game and birds, including **Saddle-billed Stork**.

■ *Going south:* The journey through the more arid southeast to the Tana River is hot and long. Check out the baobab trees for nesting buffalo weavers or **Chestnut Weaver** and visiting sunbirds and hoopoes. The *Commiphora* bush here is home to **Helmeted** and **Vulturine guineafowl**, **Eastern Yellow-billed Hornbill**, the eastern race (more commonly seen at the coast) of **Black-headed Batis**, **Broad-billed Roller**, **Rosy-patched Bushshrike**, honeyguides and orioles. **Bee-eaters** include the **Somali**, **White-throated** (Afrotropic migrant), **Blue-cheeked** (in season) and **Madagascar** (Malagasy migrant, which is known to breed along the river here). On the banks of the Tana River look for **Palm-nut Vulture**, **Violet Wood-hoopoe** and parties of **Retz's Helmetshrike**. It is also one of the best places in the country to see the large **Pel's Fishing Owl**.

OTHER WILDLIFE

The big game at Meru includes rhino, which are thriving in a rhino sanctuary within the park. The unique animals of northern Kenya – Beisa oryx, reticulated giraffe and gerenuk – are not uncommon. So too are desert warthog, caracal, lesser galago, large herds of elephant, buffalo and common waterbuck.

MWEA NATIONAL RESERVE ⁱIBA

KEY SPECIES
White-backed Night Heron, African Darter, Pel's Fishing Owl, Eastern Yellow-billed Hornbill, Hinde's Babbler (E), Yellow Wagtail.

This is a small wildlife area situated north of five dams that provide the bulk of Kenya's hydroelectric energy. The Kenyan endemic **Hinde's Babbler** and two species that are rarely seen elsewhere, **White-backed Night Heron** and **Pel's Fishing Owl**, are found at Mwea National Reserve.

HABITAT
Only 42km² in area, Mwea's bushland is dominated by a mix of *Acacia-Commiphora* and baobab trees. Thick riverine vegetation is found along the Thiba River on the reserve's northeastern boundary and along the Tana River on its southern boundary. To the southeast, at the confluence of these two rivers, lies the Kamburu Dam. *Sesbania* grow on river floodplains, while the lightly wooded grassland areas are dotted with red-pod *Terminalia brownii* (*mwalambe* in Swahili), the seeds of which turn purple as they mature.

GETTING THERE
Take Garissa Road (A3) out of Thika, driving for about 78km and passing the turn-offs to the Thika settling ponds (Site 19) and the Ol Donyo Sabuk National Park. Turn left into the road to Embu (B7) and drive for another 20km, then turn onto the rough road

signposted 'Masinga Dam Resort 12km'. The reserve is 17km beyond the resort, over the dam causeway, on a murram road that travels through areas with red and black cotton soils, both of which can be a challenge in the rainy seasons.

VISITOR INFO
Kenya Wildlife Service manages this reserve. The reserve receives relatively few visitors, so do take some time to chat with the officers at the gate about the latest happenings, and ask to borrow a map for the duration of your stay.

There are camping sites, but they have no facilities. The Masinga Dam Resort makes a reasonable alternative, and there is some excellent birding to be had on its extensive grounds.

Peter Steward

African Darter

THE BIRDING

At the Main Gate, scan above the acacias for **Little Swift** and **Lesser Striped** and **Red-rumped swallows**. **Speckled Pigeon** and **Laughing Dove** are also likely to be around.

Tracks lead from the gate through the bush and fan out to the eastern and southern waterways. **African Paradise Flycatcher**, including an unusual mixed morph, flitter between the trees. **Blue-capped Cordon-bleu** may be dashing in and out of tall grass along with **Rattling Cisticola** and **Black-cheeked Waxbill**. On seeing you, groups of **Crested Francolin** are likely stop their squeaky cackling and dash for cover.

Eastern Yellow-billed Hornbill, Rüppell's Long-tailed and **Fischer's starlings** and **Cut-throat Finch** are regularly sighted, while **Vitelline Masked, Lesser Masked** and **Village weavers** are common. Also look out for **African Cuckoo** (an Afrotropic migrant), wandering hunting parties of **White-crested Helmetshrike, Eastern Violet-backed** and **Marico sunbirds** and **Somali Bunting**.

Listen for **Hinde's Babbler** occurring in small groups in the bush along the Thiba and Upper Tana circuits. Riverside trees are the haunt of the large dusty brown **Pel's Fishing Owl**, which preys on fish. If you hear a drumming sound, its source may turn out to be a large **Bearded Woodpecker**. **African Orange-bellied Parrot, Black-headed Oriole, Zanzibar Greenbul, Red-capped Robin Chat** and **Eastern Golden Weaver** are other resident birds. **Yellow Wagtail** roost in their thousands along the Tana River in season (October–April). Migration also brings **Eurasian Bee-eater, Eurasian Golden Oriole** and **Eastern Olivaceous** and **Willow warblers**.

The dam can be reached very quickly using the Central Road. The Hippo Pools, View Point and Lodge Site (an abandoned hut) are good spots from which to look out across the water and check for a **Grey Heron** or **Great White Egret** hunting for a meal in the water on the opposite shoreline, or, in season, for graceful **White-winged Black** and **Whiskered terns** hovering over the water. **Malachite** and **Pied kingfishers** are easy to spot on the bank closest to you, as are **Reed Cormorant** and **African Darter**, which sun themselves from the bare branches of trees. Somewhat more difficult to spot are **White-backed Night** and **Striated herons**.

OTHER WILDLIFE

Side-striped squirrels scamper away at the sight of a car. Elephant are evident from their dung piles and the trees that they bring down on the tracks. Other wildlife includes buffalo, crocodile and hippo.

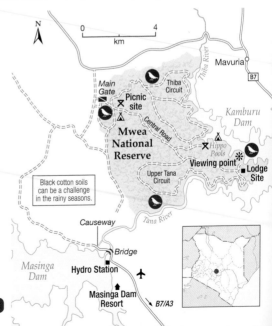

SITE 18

MWEA PADDIES

KEY SPECIES

Dwarf Bittern, Purple Swamphen, Long-toed Plover, Greater Painted-snipe, Yellow-crowned Bishop, White-winged Widowbird.

The irrigated paddy fields of Mwea are situated on the Nairobi–Embu (B6) road, 54km from Thika. They create an expansive wetland, where significant numbers of water birds, waders, seedeaters and birds of prey come to feed.

HABITAT

The paddies forming part of the Mwea Irrigation Scheme stretch over an area of black cotton soil. Grass ridges run between groups of paddies. The paddies are fed by rivers such as the Thiba, Nyamindi and others, which flow from the Aberdare mountain range and through a system of open canals. The National Irrigation Board periodically allows the canal gates to be opened so that the rivers can flood the fields. Scrub

grows intermittently along the canals and includes beautiful candle bush trees with their glowing yellow flowers.

GETTING THERE

Take the Thika Road (A2) from Nairobi past the towns of Thika, Kabiti, Kenol and Makuyu. When you reach Makutano, travel east on the B6 for 8.5km and you'll have reached the first of the rice fields.

VISITOR INFO

The main road (B6) abuts the paddies, providing a good vantage point. You'll need to find safe places to get off the road. The best times to visit are in the migration season, October–April. Rice mills are located in the same area, so aromatic Kenya Pishori rice is readily available for purchase in towns nearby.

Dwarf Bittern

Yellow-crowned Bishop

THE BIRDING

Workers and owners do not usually object to your walking on the grassy strips between the rows of paddies. Here you get good views over the paddies, which typically host herons, whistling ducks, **Little Grebe**, **Great White** and **Yellow-billed egrets** and **Black Crake**.

A pair of Greater Painted-snipe

Foraging in the water and on the grassy verges, **Yellow-billed**, **African Open-billed**, **Abdim's** (Afrotropic migrant) and **White storks** (in season) can be plentiful. Large flocks of **Grey Crowned Crane** also occur. Look more closely for **Long-toed** and **Three-banded plovers**, **Marsh**, **Wood** and **Common sandpipers** and **Common Greenshank** picking invertebrates from the mud. You may also spot **Little** and **Dwarf bitterns**, **Purple Swamphen** and **Greater Painted-snipe** partly hidden by the weeds and grass.

Working the paddies there may be **Long-crested Eagle**, **Lanner Falcon** and, in season, **Western Marsh Harrier**. A speciality here, looking and behaving in flight almost like the giant European bumblebee, is the black-and-yellow **Yellow-crowned Bishop**. **Diederik Cuckoo**, **Wattled Starling** and **White-winged Widowbird** stop on the scrub, while lower down within the foliage there may be **Black-crowned Night Heron**.

Other birds seen here are **Glossy Ibis**, **African Spoonbill**, **Whiskered Tern**, **Plain Martin**, **Lesser Striped Swallow** and, in season, **Barn Swallow** and **Common House Martin**. Quelea can descend in their thousands at harvest time, causing considerable problems for farmers.

OTHER WILDLIFE

In and around the rice paddies there are amphibians and reptiles including lizards, as well as insects such as grasshoppers, dragonflies and beetles.

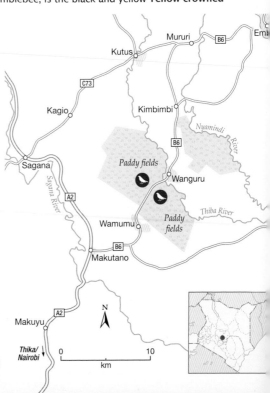

THIKA SETTLING PONDS

KEY SPECIES

Hottentot Teal, Southern Pochard. **Passage migrants:** Northern Shoveler, Northern Pintail, Garganey, Ferruginous Duck.

Outside the town of Thika lies a series of oxidation ponds used for sewage-water treatment. Sewage enters them continuously, and they receive plenty of sunlight, making them an ideal breeding ground for large numbers of insects and microorganisms. As a result, the ponds are especially rich feeding grounds for a wide variety of bird species, including large numbers of migrating waders and ducks.

HABITAT

The concrete settling ponds, which carry varying quantities of waste water, take up most of the site, but there are grass embankments between the ponds. As you walk along these embankments you will find a few scattered *Acacia* trees, the odd Nandi flame *Spathodea campanulata* and some opportunistic plants like Sodom apple *Solanum incanum* and sedge.

GETTING THERE

Unfortunately, to get to the ponds you will have to pass through Thika's rubbish dump. From Thika, take the Garissa Road east to the crowded settlement of Makongeni. At Makongeni take a right onto the road leading to the post office, which you will be able to see from the main road. Continue along this dusty track until it reaches a T-junction, where you will turn left. Drive along this dirt track for 2.4km (keeping to the right after 1km) and you will pass through a swampy stretch and the rubbish dump. Turn right again to the sewage ponds.

VISITOR INFO

The Thika Water and Sewerage Company manages the works, and access is not usually a problem. Request permission by email (**thikawater@yahoo.com**) before going to the site.

Peter Usher

The Kenya Rufous Sparrow is often seen perched on a shrub when not feeding on the ground.

THE BIRDING

The big stars are the migratory ducks, which are easy to observe at these open rectangular ponds. In season, October–April, **Northern Shoveler**, **Northern Pintail**, **Garganey** and **Ferruginous Duck** can occur. They favour the cleaner ponds further down the site where there is less sewage and where they mingle with common pond residents like **Little Grebe** and **Black Crake**. Ducks that are regularly seen include **Fulvous Whistling**, **White-backed**, **Knob-billed** and **Yellow-billed ducks**, **Red-billed Teal**, **Hottentot Teal** and **Southern Pochard**.

The first few ponds are heavy with sludge and more popular with **Black-winged Stilt** and plovers (**Long-toed**, **Blacksmith**, **Spur-winged** and **Three-banded**) and, in season, **Little Ringed Plover**, sandpipers, **Little** and **Temminck's stints** and **Ruff**, which may be found feeding in the sludge or picking insects from the sloping sides of the ponds.

Malachite Kingfisher and **Reed Cormorant** may be seen on the sides of drainage outlets in these ponds. Among patches of sedge and scrub, look out for **Winding** and **Stout cisticolas**, **Black-crowned Night Heron**, **Great Reed** and **Dark-capped Yellow warblers**, **Kenya Rufous Sparrow** and small numbers of **Red-billed Quelea**.

OTHER WILDLIFE

Monitor lizards may surprise you at these ponds.

Peter Usher

Garganey, Yellow-billed Duck and Red-billed Teal

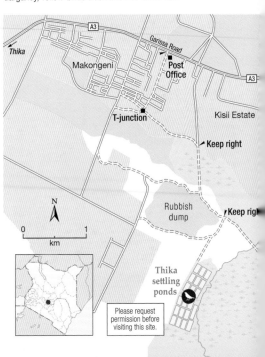

SITE 20

MAGADI ROAD

KEY SPECIES
Pringle's Puffback, Ashy Cisticola, Wailing Cisticola, Scaly Chatterer, Beautiful Sunbird, Steel-blue Whydah, Southern Grosbeak Canary.

This amazing 100km drive starts from Nairobi, traverses the Ngong Hills at an altitude of 2,130m and descends to Lake Magadi, at 606m. It is one of the hottest places in Kenya. The Maasai have long grazed their cattle in the country along the Magadi Road, and few other activities occur there, although, increasingly, houses are being constructed. The road was originally built to serve the former Magadi Soda Company and is relatively lightly used. The open countryside and the easy road make it possible to seek out the 500 or more different bird species.

HABITAT
The drive descends from the wetter highlands near Nairobi to the dry lava plains, soda deposits and hot springs of Lake Magadi and beyond. Open woodlands alternate with grassland and areas of scrub. Here, there are many acacias and *Delonix elata*, while *Commiphora* are noticeable on the hillsides, together with marvellous succulent plants, including stands of sansevieria, and *Euphorbia*. Since the landscape is dry for much of the year, birds are attracted to seasonal swamps, rivers and watering holes, which therefore make excellent birding spots along the way.

GETTING THERE
To reach the town of Magadi, go past Olorgesailie (see directions for Site 21) and stay on the Magadi Road (C58) for another 45km, passing the Ol Ndyokie volcano on your left.

VISITOR INFO
The road was full of potholes, but roadworks are in progress. Corner Baridi can be cold and windy, while Magadi is hot and harsh. Fees are due at Olorgesailie and at Magadi for access to the hot springs. Individual Maasai may attempt to charge you for stopping here so it is best to stick to birding along the road, on tracks or at places like the Olorgesailie museum site. At Lake Magadi, Tata Chemicals Magadi has mining operations and a factory, and controls access to the town of Magadi. The security officers at the entry barrier will want some details about you and your visit, but there is no charge for entry.

Take plenty of water and make sure you have fuel: there are no petrol stations on the Magadi Road from Nairobi, and you will only be able to fill up at Magadi. You can also seek out the Flamingo Club in the north of the town and the Magadi Sports Club (on Shompole Road in the south) for cold drinks. Camp sites and bandas are available for hire at the site of the Olorgesailie Museum, while at Magadi you can stay at the tented camp or in one of the few rooms available at the club (lakemagadi.com).

The view from Magadi Road

THE BIRDING

■ *Corner Baridi:* This is at the top of the road cresting the Ngong Hills, before you descend the escarpment. It overlooks grass and bush with a scattering of homes and a stunning view of the rift dotted with volcanos. Spend some time here or turn left onto the dirt track along Champagne Ridge. **Abyssinian** (or Schalow's) **Wheatear** is easily seen out in the open, and **Speke's Weaver** is heard from the trees. Short grass and scrub along the Champagne Ridge track can yield **Red-capped** and **Short-tailed larks, Wailing Cisticola, Brown Parisoma, Little Rock Thrush, Grassland Pipit** and **Reichenow's Seedeater.** Check any flowering *Leonotis* for **Scarlet-chested, Bronze, Golden-winged, Beautiful, Marico** or **Variable sunbirds.** Migrants in season (October–April) may include **Isabelline** and **Northern wheatears.**

■ *After Kisamese:* Descend from the Corner Baridi viewpoint and drive past the town of Kisamese. You may wish to detour up to an exposed ridge on the left, which leads to the Olepolos Country Club, and scan for **White-necked Raven.** Back on the Magadi Road, you will descend through a gorge (often passing trucks struggling with the ascent back to Nairobi). Look out alongside the road here for **Scaly Chatterer** as well as **Pringle's Puffback** (an undescribed form found only here).

After another 2km you will find a dirt track going left at the signposts for Sintato Mixed Secondary School and the Tanathi Water Services Board – this area is perhaps Kenya's most reliable locality for **Southern Grosbeak Canary.** Other resident birds include **Temminck's Courser, Rufous-crowned Roller, Red-fronted Barbet, Nubian Woodpecker, Brown-crowned Tchagra,**

Red-fronted Barbet

Wenfat Tong

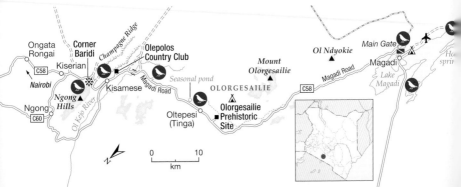

Slate-coloured Boubou, **Rattling** and (uncommon) **Tiny cisticolas, Yellow-bellied Eremomela, Banded Parisoma, White-bellied Canary** and **Cinnamon-breasted Bunting**. Keep an eye out for raptors, which may include the **Lesser Kestrel** (in season), **Lanner Falcon, Brown Snake Eagle, Eastern Chanting Goshawk, Verreaux's Eagle** and vultures.

■ *Beyond Ol Kejo River:* Look out for **Taita Fiscal** and **Ashy Cisticola** as you continue on the road after the river, for about 10km, to reach another track to the left. Among the acacias there are other resident birds, including several species of cuckoo (especially after rains), **Black-throated Barbet, Mouse-coloured Penduline Tit,**

Yellow-bellied Eremomela

Black-cheeked Waxbill, Cut-throat Finch, up to four species of whydah, including the **Steel-blue Whydah,** and **Somali Bunting**. In season (October–April) any number of Palaearctic migrants can also be found, including **Isabelline** and **Lesser Grey shrikes, Eastern Olivaceous** and **Willow warblers, Common Whitethroat, Irania** and **Common Rock Thrush**. Except in the harshest places, congregations of **Abdim's** (an Afrotropic migrant) and **Black** and **White storks** might be seen in any expanse of grassland along this road.

A couple of kilometres before Oltepesi there is a small seasonal pond on the left of the road, which is a good spot for doves, **Red-billed Quelea,** numerous waxbills, **Vitelline Masked** and **Chestnut weavers** and, after good rains, **Fire-fronted Bishop**.

■ *Oltepesi (Tinga):* The **Grey-headed** (Swahili) **Sparrow** roves around the village of Oltepesi and **White-throated Bee-eater** are present from September to April, although a few may breed in the area. The older of the two watering tanks, which has a small wet area around it, is now refurbished and is often very busy with goatherds watering their flocks and the activities of an expanding village.

About 3km beyond Oltepesi lies the Olorgesailie Prehistoric Site (see Site 21), and another 47km further on, the lake for which the road was named – Lake Magadi (see Site 22).

OTHER WILDLIFE

The road cuts through a huge expanse of land in which you are more likely to see large numbers of Maasai cattle grazing than any other big mammals. That is not to say there is no game, however. You may see Kirk's dik-dik and hear the whooping calls of hyena or jackal at night. Lesser kudu may still reside in the hills that you pass along the way.

OLORGESAILIE PREHISTORIC SITE

KEY SPECIES
Double-banded Courser, Horus Swift, Red-and-yellow Barbet, Fawn-coloured Lark, Ashy Cisticola, Tiny Cisticola, Blue-capped Cordon-bleu, Grey-capped Social Weaver, Somali Bunting.

Situated in semi-arid country 65km southwest of Nairobi, the Olorgesailie Prehistoric Site is a favourite with birders during the dreary days of the cold season (July, August and September) in Nairobi. The drive there is one of the most scenic routes in the country, with an exciting diversity of thornbush birds.

HABITAT
The site and its environs are dominated by grass and scattered acacia bush, including *Acacia tortilis* and the 'wait-a-bit thorn' *A. mellifera*. They grow on white silica sediments made up of the skeletons of algae deposited during repeated floods that took place in ancient times in the Olorgesailie area. The poisonous milkweed *Calotropis procera* dots the landscape, which is scarred by overgrazing and charcoal logging.

GETTING THERE
From Nairobi turn into Magadi Road at the Bomas of Kenya roundabout, before the Galleria Shopping Mall, and drive towards the extended sprawl of Ongata

The semi-arid bush area where the archaeological site of Olorgesailie is found

Rongai and Kiserian. After these towns, you will reach the open green slopes of the Ngong Hills, ascend to Corner Baridi and then begin to descend the long route to the floor of the Southern Rift Valley in Kenya. Be wary of cows, goats and donkeys, which sometimes wander onto the road.

The descent is more than 1,000m, and the road is currently very potholed. It passes the extinct volcano Ol'Doinyo Esakut and ends below Mount Olorgesailie. En route you will pass the towns of Kisamese and Olepolos and a number of villages. The road ascends, and 3km after Oltepesi (also called Tinga) you'll be at the turn-off signposted for the Olorgesailie Prehistoric Site. Turn left and drive for another 1.5km along a white dust road, which subsequently veers left into the site.

VISITOR INFO
This archaeological site is well known for the large number of hand axes, other stone artefacts and animal fossils found here. It consists of a small museum building and covered excavation sites and is open throughout the year. An entry fee is levied, although it is smaller if you intend only to use the picnic banda. You can book overnight accommodation at the camping site or bandas via the National Museums of Kenya (**publicrelations@museums. or.ke**), but facilities are basic, and you'll need to bring your own food, cooking equipment and bedding. It can get very hot, so bring plenty of drinking (and cooking) water.

THE BIRDING

The 1.5km of hot dusty white road that leads into Olorgesailie is normally quite unattractive to birds, but becomes more interesting when migrants arrive in season, October–April. In the bush further down the road look out for **Isabelline** and **Lesser Grey shrikes**, **Eastern Olivaceous**, **Willow** and **Garden warblers**, **Capped** and **Pied wheatears** and **Spotted Flycatcher**.

■ *Around the museum site:* A trail meanders around the gently sloping site. It takes you from the reception and the small museum building, past the excavations, back up along the top perimeter behind the newer bandas and ends at the picnic banda. A walk along this route is likely to produce **Fawn-coloured Lark**, **Ashy Cisticola**, **Banded Parisoma**, **Eastern Violet-backed** and **Scarlet-chested sunbirds**, **Chestnut Sparrow**, **Somali Bunting** and **Cinnamon-breasted Bunting**.

In the trees and bushes along the perimeter hedge there may be **White-bellied Go-away Bird**, **Blue-naped Mousebird**, **Spot-flanked** and **Red-and-yellow barbets** and, low in the undergrowth, **Spotted Palm Thrush** and **White-browed Scrub Robin**.

■ *Riverside:* From the museum building go past the older bandas, to the left of the museum, checking for **Grey-capped Social Weaver** and **Vitelline Masked Weaver** that nest in the acacias. Regular predators at these weaver nests include **Gabar Goshawk**, **African Harrier Hawk**, **Eastern Chanting Goshawk** and **Diederik Cuckoo**.

Beat a path through the grassland en route to the large *lugga* that runs parallel to the main road and east of the site. Besides bustards and whydahs, birds that may be seen include **Double-banded** and **Heuglin's** (uncommon) **coursers**, **Rufous-crowned Roller**, **White-throated Bee-eater** (September–April), **African Grey** and **Red-billed hornbills**, **Taita Fiscal**, **Abyssinian Wheatear** (also known as Schalow's Wheatear) and **Red-billed Quelea**. You also have a good chance of spotting **Horus Swift** overhead, **Singing Bush Lark** in the wet months, **Fischer's Sparrow Lark** and, in season, **Common Rock Thrush**.

The riparian acacia scrub here, and on the smaller seasonal river below the museum, can host **Nubian Woodpecker**, **Red-throated Tit**, **Tiny Cisticola**, **Red-fronted Warbler**, **Grey Wren Warbler**, **Yellow-bellied Eremomela**, **Northern Crombec**, **Yellow-spotted Petronia** and the **Southern Grosbeak** and **White-bellied canaries**.

Peter Usher

The dark morph Gabar Goshawk is not uncommon and may be found together with the more common grey bird.

Jacques Pitteloud

D'Arnaud's Barbet

■ **Picnic banda:** The picnic banda is well positioned a short distance from some acacias and right beside a floor-level birdbath shaded by some bush. Empty a little water in the birdbath in the dry months and several birds that can be found around the site will approach.

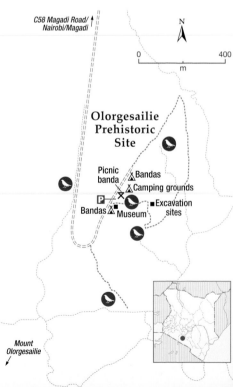

These may include **D'Arnaud's Barbet**, **Crimson-rumped** and **Black-cheeked waxbills**, **Blue-capped Cordon-bleu**, **Green-winged Pytilia**, **Cut-throat Finch** and **Grey-headed** and **African silverbills**.

Aim to arrive at Olorgesaillie the evening before you intend birding so that you can get an early start in the morning, before the heat of the day sets in. If you hear nightjars calling, they are likely to be **Donaldson-Smith's** or **Slender-tailed nightjars**.

OTHER WILDLIFE

While the fossil record indicates that wildlife was once abundant at Olorgesailie, this is no longer the case, although you may see or hear those animals mentioned under Site 20, Magadi Road – such as dik-dik, hyena and jackal.

C58 Magadi Road/ Nairobi/Magadi

N

0   400
m

Olorgesailie Prehistoric Site

Picnic banda
Bandas
Camping grounds
P
Bandas
Museum
Excavation sites

Mount Olorgesailie

LAKE MAGADI IBA

KEY SPECIES

Cape Teal, Lesser Flamingo, African Spoonbill, Pied Avocet, Black-winged Stilt, Chestnut-banded Plover. **Passage migrants:** Little Stint.

Lake Magadi lies at the lowest point of the Southern Rift Valley in Kenya. In the baking heat sulphur fumes evaporate rapidly from the soda ash lake. Fed by hot springs, the water sometimes looks pink or red, owing to halophilic (salt-loving) bacteria. In the shallow brackish lagoons around the lake tilapia *Alcolapia graham* and algae survive. They attract flamingos, pelicans, herons, storks and waders. **Chestnut-banded Plover** is reliably common at Lake Magadi.

HABITAT

This is a landscape of ancient lake deposits dotted with thornbush.

GETTING THERE

Lake Magadi is at the end of Magadi Road, a little less than 45km beyond the turn-off leading to the Olorgesailie Prehistoric site. For more details, see Site 21.

VISITOR INFO

Birds occur at the many lagoons around the lake. The most accessible lagoons are close to the Main Gate and near to the hot springs

in the south and southwest. The Lake Magadi area falls under the management of the Tata Chemicals Magadi Company, which mines soda ash here. To visit the hot springs an entry fee is payable at the reception of the Magadi Sports Club. Once you have paid, continue on the road south after the Magadi Sports Club. Very soon thereafter the road merges with a series of dirt tracks. Drive to the left and then south onto the track that goes past the ghost of what was once the town's golf course and past the airstrip on your right. After about 8km the track will start veering right towards the hot springs (about another 7km away). The approach to the hot springs skirts the southern lagoons and goes across the lake's floodplain. It is passable only when conditions have been dry. If it has rained, trying to cross the floodplain without getting stuck in the sediment is a gamble you are likely to lose. If you are determined, you can better your chances by asking for a guide when you pay to enter at the Club. For more on road conditions, fees and accommodation, see Site 20.

The lagoons southwest of Lake Magadi are best visited during the dry seasons.

Lake Magadi and Amboseli National Park are good places to look for Chestnut-banded Plover.

THE BIRDING

Greater Flamingo, thousands of **Lesser Flamingo** and good numbers of **Great White** and **Pink-backed pelicans,** herons, storks, waders and **Chestnut-banded Plover** can be found in the pools beside the 250m stretch of road leading to the security barrier operated by Tata Chemicals Magadi.

Other birds are **Red-billed** and **Cape teals, Yellow-billed Stork, African Spoonbill, Little** and **Dimorphic egrets** and **Black-winged Stilt. Pied Avocet** and **Collared Pratincole** are known to breed at Lake Magadi. In season (October–April) **Kittlitz's Plover, Little Stint, Ruff** and **Curlew Sandpiper** feed here, **Grey-headed Gull** flock at the lakeshore and **White-winged Black Tern** dip and dive for food.

Similar lagoons with equally good birding occur to the south and southwest of the lake, where there are also hot springs.

OTHER WILDLIFE

With some luck you may spot zebra or wildebeest near the hot springs, or giraffe and gerenuk in grassland around the lake.

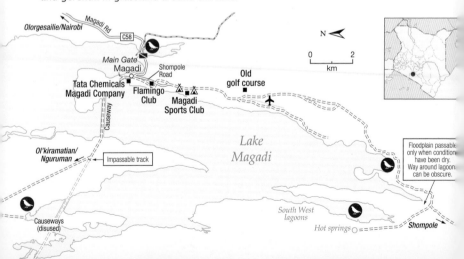

Olorgesailie/Nairobi

Magadi Rd

C58

Main Gate
Magadi

Shompole Road

Old golf course

Tata Chemicals Magadi Company

Flamingo Club

Magadi Sports Club

Causeway

N

0   2
km

Ol'kiramatian/ Nguruman   Impassable track

Lake Magadi

Floodplain passable only when conditions have been dry. Way around lagoon can be obscure.

Causeways (disused)

South West lagoons

Hot springs

Shompole

NGURUMAN IBA

KEY SPECIES
Black-fronted Bushshrike, Desert Cisticola, Black Bishop, Southern Red Bishop, Jackson's Widowbird.

Nguruman is a hot arid wilderness that is well off the beaten track and far from any big towns. The area consists of a number of ranches belonging to the Maasai community. The region is in southern Kenya, west of Lake Magadi and below the Nguruman Escarpment, which forms part of the western wall of the Rift Valley. Birds that are common south of the Kenyan–Tanzanian border, such as **Southern Red Bishop**, reach their northern range limits here. Close to the escarpment and extending to the border are the Ol'kiramatian and Shompole group ranches.

HABITAT
The southern Ewaso Ng'iro River runs east of the Ol'kiramatian Group Ranch and southwards towards the border. Here it enters the extensive Engare Ng'iro swamp, which drains into Lake Natron in Tanzania. The wooded slopes of the Nguruman Escarpment, with their springs, cascading streams and waterfalls, give way to plains, which are a mosaic of dry thornbush and grassland, with some woodland along the Oloibortoto, Entasopia, Sampu and other rivers. The small trading town of Ol'kiramatian serves the needs of the wider Maasai community and a small number of farmers tilling the northwestern corner of the ranch. Nguruman is an incredibly beautiful area, with views of both the steep-sided Shompole Mountain at the border and the still-active Lengai volcano in Tanzania.

GETTING THERE
Travelling west from the entry to the Magadi area to the other side of Lake Magadi means using the Magadi Causeway. From the Tata Chemicals Magadi Company security barrier veer to the right at the junction where the road crests and go around the north end of the soda ash factory. Note that navigating the causeway requires some careful driving, and it may not be possible to use it if the rains have been heavy.

The road forks soon after the causeway. The original track, which continues straight ahead, is not usable. Instead take the right-hand track and continue as the road loops around for 15km before joining the original track going west. It is rocky, and your progress is likely to be slow. After 5.5km you'll see a track to the left, which, if you wish to take a detour, goes through wooded grassland, with some wildlife, including gerenuk, and ends at an old disused causeway. Here there are lagoons that you can scan for birds.

The woodlands, plains and mountains west and south of Lake Magadi can be seen from the Nguruman Escarpment.

Continue on the looping road, which meets the original track going west, bears right and continues west for another 12km, passing through some incredibly dry country, to reach the bridge over the Ewaso Ng'iro River. The Lale'enok Resource Centre is located a few metres before the bridge. Guides are available here, and you can pay the conservancy fee (otherwise, pay at the gate). Turn left after the bridge and soon you will pass through the Ol'kiramatian Conservancy Gate, which is currently under construction.

The alternative route is to go via the southern hot springs and avoid the rocky road in the north, but the track is rather

THE BIRDING

Yellow-throated Sandgrouse and **Fischer's Sparrow Lark** are common and will be seen feeding on the road en route. Also look in the bush alongside the road for **Abyssinian Scimitarbill**, **Red-fronted Warbler**, typically seen holding its very long tail upright, and **Yellow-spotted Petronia**. Cross the bridge over the Ewaso Ng'iro to explore the road for a wide variety of birds. You may hear the sounds of **Rufous Chatterer** and **Arrow-marked Babbler** and, especially in the mornings, the sweet singing of **Spotted Palm Thrush** emanating from thickets of *Salvadora persica*, known locally as *msuake*. **Grey-headed Sparrow** and numerous doves may be seen perched or feeding from the ground. In the west, there are trails that the local Maasai follow to travel from the lower slopes to the top of the escarpment and beyond. Here, you may find the uncommon **Grey-crested Helmetshrike**, which favours *Tarchonanthus* or *leleshwa* bushes.

Returning to the Ewaso Ng'iro bridge and the conservancy gate, there is a track heading south, parallel to the Ewaso Ng'iro, and another going southwest towards the escarpment (with a directional signpost to Lentorre Lodge). Start on either track, looking out for **Striped** and **Woodland kingfishers**, **Black-fronted Bushshrike**, **Rüppell's Starling** and **Black-necked** (uncommon) and **Vitelline Masked weavers**.

Bare-faced Go-away-bird

Spotted Thick-knee

obscure, has sections of deep soft sand and should be attempted only in dry conditions or with a local guide.

VISITOR INFO

Nguruman lacks the routes and tourist facilities that are familiar at most parks. If you intend camping, careful planning and a high degree of self-sufficiency are required. Bear in mind that there are large troops of baboons in the area, that tsetse fly can sometimes be a nuisance and that the tracks can be very dusty. Alternatively, Lentorre Lodge (www.lentorre.com), situated below the escarpment but above the plains, provides more luxurious accommodation.

In the acacia bush around Lentorre Lodge you may find **Bare-faced Go-away-bird**, which seems to have expanded its range into this part of the south from moister areas nearer Lake Victoria.

In more sparsely wooded grasslands look for **Kori Bustard**, **Spotted Thick-knee**, **Double-banded** and **Heuglin's coursers**, **Gull-billed Tern**, **Zitting Cisticola**, **Desert Cisticola** and **Jackson's Widowbird**. Also look out for the bishops – the stunning **Fire-fronted Bishop**, the uncommon **Black Bishop** and the **Southern Red Bishop**, which is at the very northernmost point of its range here. When the grass is high, you could surprise a female **Ostrich** incubating as many as 24 eggs or more or, in season (October–April), catch a fleeting glance of the threatened **Corncrake**. After good rains storks may be out in their hundreds hunting for termites, while in season various migrant shrikes and chats may also be present.

OTHER WILDLIFE

In addition to the wildlife mentioned under Site 20 (Magadi Road), cheetah, lion, leopard, bat-eared fox, aardwolf and porcupine are seen here. Elephant also come down along a migratory corridor from the Loita Hills.

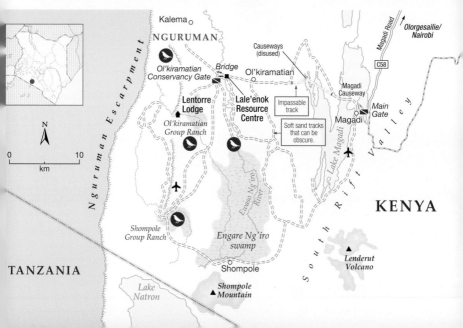

LAKE NAIVASHA IBA

KEY SPECIES
Eurasian Teal, Great Crested Grebe, Black Heron, Spotted Redshank, Temminck's Stint, Black-headed Gull, Lesser Black-backed Gull, White-fronted Bee-eater, Wahlberg's Honeybird.

A shallow freshwater lake on the floor of the Rift Valley, Lake Navaisha is located 80km northwest of Nairobi and is one of the most beautiful of Kenya's Rift Valley lakes. It is set in a basin with the Kinangop Plateau to the east, the volcanic Mount Longonot to the south, the Mau Escarpment to the west and the Eburru Mountains to the north. It is a spectacular birding destination, with over 150 resident and migrant wetland species. Hippo Camp on the eastern lakeshore is a particularly productive birding spot.

Jacques Pitteloud

Little Egret

HABITAT
Lake Naivasha lies at an altitude of 1,890m. Water hyacinth *Eichhornia crassipes* and other floating invasives occur to varying extents on the lake. In places it is fringed with papyrus *Cyperus papyrus*, while attractive stands of yellow fever trees *Acacia xanthophloea* grow in undisturbed ground around it. Water flows into Naivasha from underground and from the Malewa River, which drains the Aberdare range, but the lake has no surface outlet. Its maximum depth averages about 8m, but it incorporates a submerged volcanic crater, Crescent Island Lagoon, with depths of up to 17m.

GETTING THERE
Turn off the A104 from Nairobi before the Naivasha overpass and travel down Moi Avenue and, subsequently, Moi South Lake Road for about 4km. Look out for the Hippo Camp sign on your right.

VISITOR INFO
There are many lakeside resorts and camps, but access may be determined by whether you are booked to stay. Hippo Camp is managed by the Kenya Wildlife Service. It offers excellent birding. Mention at the gate that you would like to bird-watch at the lake's edge, and ask for details of any wildlife in the area.

Eunice Ngarachu

Where *Acacia* woodlands survive around Lake Navaisha they hold a rich variety of birds including cuckoos, barbets and honeyguides.

THE BIRDING

After you've paid at the Hippo Camp Gate it is a short drive to the end of the track that stops before the causeway. You can leave your vehicle and look around at the lake's edge, depending on the water level, but be careful of wild animals, especially hippos.

When the water level is low, the exposed mud flats may host a stunning variety of waders, ducks and other water birds, including grebes, ibises, spoonbills, herons, egrets, stilts and avocets. In season (October–April) **Black-tailed Godwit**, **Spotted Redshank**, **Common Greenshank, Temminck's Stint** and **Ruff** may also be seen. Pelicans, comorants, **Black-headed Gull** and, increasingly, **Lesser Black-backed Gull** may also be found resting on the causeway. **Cape Teal** and **Southern Pochard** may be numerous, **African Water Rail** may lurk among the reeds and other plants at the lake's edge, while **Yellow-billed Duck** and **Common Moorhen** may be seen swimming and feeding.

Less common species regularly found here include the **Black Heron**, which hunts by forming an 'umbrella' with its wings, casting shade to which small fish are attracted, and **Great Crested Grebe**, East Africa's most endangered water bird. Among the migrant ducks on the lake there may be **Garganey**, **Northern Pintail** and **Shoveler** and, less commonly, **Eurasian Teal**.

On the way back from the lake, **White-fronted Bee-eater** may be seen in the acacias. **Grey-backed Fiscal**, **Black-lored Babbler**, **Common Stonechat**, **Moorland Chat**, **Plain-backed Pipit** and several cuckoo species are found in the open trees and scrub. Both **Wahlberg's Honeybird** and **Grey-rumped Swallow** are regularly seen here, as, in season, are various migrant shrikes, warblers and the **Yellow Wagtail**.

OTHER WILDLIFE

Among the large mammals found around the lake's edge there may be impala, zebra, giraffe and waterbuck. Do not approach the wildlife and take special care when there are buffalo. Although hippos are normally offshore during the day, they can turn up unexpectedly too.

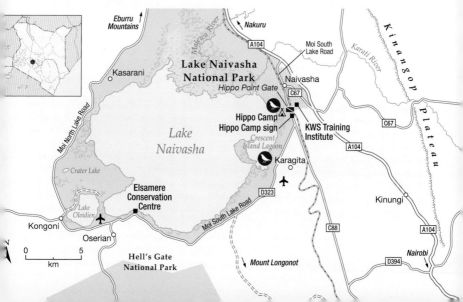

LAKE ELEMENTAITA IBA

KEY SPECIES

Great Crested Grebe, Greater Flamingo, Lesser Flamingo, African Spoonbill, Great White Pelican, Crowned Eagle, Pied Avocet, Southern Ground Hornbill, Grey-crested Helmetshrike, Jackson's Widowbird.

Lake Elementaita doesn't get the same attention as the larger lakes Naivasha and Nakuru, but it is amazingly beautiful. It is shallow and alkaline with abundant quantities of blue-green algae that attract **Lesser Flamingo**. The rivers and hot springs in the area also provide sufficient water to encourage the **Great White Pelican** to breed.

HABITAT

The lake varies in extent depending on the inflow from the Mbaruk, Chamuka and Meroroni rivers. It averages 15–20km² in area, but has at times been close to drying up entirely. Hot springs on the lake's southeast shore empty into Elementaita and are an important source of nutrients. The vegetation is similar to that at Lake Nakuru (Site 26). Acacia woodlands grow close to the lake, while beyond this, much of the surrounding landscape consists of dry plains. To the

south lie the volcanic cones and craters of the Elementaita badlands. They include a split crater nicknamed the 'Sleeping Warrior' and the Horseshoe Crater, nicknamed 'Delamere's Nose' on account of their shapes when seen from a distance.

GETTING THERE

From Naivasha stay on the Nairobi–Nakuru Road (A104) and pass the Gilgil weighbridge, the toll station and the turn-off to the town of Gilgil. The road descends and you will see Lake Elementaita on the horizon to your left. After about 31km you will reach the southern tip of the lake and the place known as Kekopey, where grilled meat (*nyama-choma*) is sold, just off the A104.

The A104 goes past the lake, which is accessible via various properties at its shores, the largest of which is the Soysambu Conservancy. To reach it

The view from Sunbird Lodge looking towards Soysambu Conservancy

you will need to drive for 12km from Kekopey. Pass the turning to Sunbird Lodge and exit onto the track on your right. Loop around by driving for 100m, turning right, driving for another 400m, turning right again and then passing under the A104 and continuing to the Main Gate. The sign indicating the turn-off to Sunbird Lodge is 8.5km from the Kekopey area.

VISITOR INFO

Soysambu Conservancy (www. soysambuconservancy.org) is a wildlife sanctuary and cattle ranch that encompasses the area to the north and west of the lake. An entry fee is payable. The hot springs in the southwest can be reached by way of a track in the south that starts near the *nyama-choma* eateries just off the A104.

THE BIRDING

■ **Kekopey area:** If you exit the A104 highway at the Kekopey area and journey for 5km along a dirt track to the hot springs, you can get a close view of beautiful congregations of **Greater** and **Lesser flamingos** and large groups of **Great White Pelican** bathing in pools or herding fish in the lake. It is also a good place to see **Yellow-billed Stork** and **African Spoonbill**, which may be present in significant numbers in the water just offshore. Look for **Black-winged Stilt** and **Pied Avocet** foraging in the water and

Great White Pelican

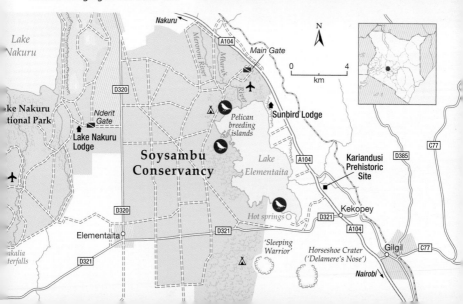

Southern Ground Hornbill

Martial Eagle

Great Crested Grebe

for families of **Yellow-billed Duck**, **Cape Teal** and **Red-knobbed Coot** swimming in the deeper water beyond.

■ *Soysambu Conservancy:* At the opposite end of the lake, in the Soysambu Conservancy, there are acacia woodlands that offer birding opportunities similar to those at Lake Nakuru. Species found here include **Greater Honeyguide**, **Arrow-marked Babbler**, the uncommon **Grey-crested Helmetshrike** and pairs of **Southern Ground Hornbill**. From the tops of the acacias and euphorbias, Martial, **Long-crested** and **Crowned eagles** scan for any movement below and, in season, **Western Marsh** and **Montagu's harriers** and **Greater Spotted** and **Steppe eagles** comb the lake.

Follow the tracks to get close to the shore and scan the lake nearby for ducks, waders and, possibly, a **Great Crested Grebe**. It is also not uncommon to spot ibises and egrets (including the **Great White Egret**) hunting intently in the shallows.

After rain, the lush grasses on the plains surrounding the lake may present opportunities to see widowbirds (**Fan-tailed**, **Red-collared**, **Long-tailed** and **Jackson's**) in their splendid breeding plumage. Listen for the easily recognized and wonderfully haunting call of the **Grey Crowned Crane** coming in to land.

■ *Sunbird Lodge:* This lodge is located up on the cliffs above the northeastern lakeshore (www.sunbirdkenya.com). From here the views are amazing, and you can watch large flocks of flamingos move like waves on the lake. This is an excellent site for swifts (**Mottled**, **Nyanza**, **Little**, **Horus** and **White-rumped**), swallows (**Barn** in season, **Lesser Striped** and **Red-rumped**), starlings, **Little Rock Thrush** and sunbirds.

OTHER WILDLIFE

Large mammals that are conspicuous around the lake include Rothschild's giraffe, waterbuck, buffalo, eland, zebra and baboon.

LAKE NAKURU 🅸🅱🅰

KEY SPECIES
Cape Teal, Black-necked Grebe, Lesser Flamingo, Western Reef Heron, Blue-spotted Wood Dove, Red-throated Wryneck, Grey-crested Helmetshrike, African Thrush.

Lake Nakuru lies to the south of the town of Nakuru, in Kenya's Rift Valley. Shallow and highly alkaline, it is renowned for huge flocks of **Lesser Flamingo**, which at times are known to have exceeded a million birds. The lake was gazetted as a bird sanctuary in 1960, the first of its kind in Africa. Today, the Lake Nakuru National Park measures 188km² and offers non-stop birding – more than 450 bird species have been recorded here.

HABITAT
The lake lies at an altitude of 1,756m, the lowest point between the Mau Escarpment in the west and the highlands in the east. Four seasonal rivers drain into it. In the northeast it is fed by springs, and here you'll find woodland and marshes with flatsedge *Cyperus* growing in the shallows. The park's vegetation is typified by *Tarchonanthus* bush, known as *leleshwa*, and by dry forest, dominated by yellow fever trees *Acacia xanthophloea*

at the lake margins, marvellous *Euphorbia candelabrum* on Sirrkon 'Lion' Hill and wild olive *Olea africana* on the southwestern escarpment.

GETTING THERE
Take the A104 highway from Nairobi to Nakuru. The park's Main Gate is 4km south of the A104 and to reach it you will have to go through Nakuru. Several roads lead to the Main Gate. Depending on traffic it is perhaps best to come off the A104 at the second roundabout directly into Kenyatta Avenue. Drive until you reach Moi Road on the right. Turn into Moi and travel south for 1km to where the road links with Flamingo Road on your left. Turn into Flamingo and carry on south, passing the Afraha Stadium on your right, and continue all the way down to the Main Gate.

To get to the Lanet Gate, leave the A104 just as it becomes a dual carriageway headed for Nakuru town. (The distance to the gate is 1.5km.)

It is possible to get close to the shores of Lake Nakuru to look for birds.

Lake Nakuru is managed by Kenya Wildlife Service and an entry fee is payable. Note that in recent years, water levels in the Rift Valley's lakes have risen, and tracks may be diverted or even closed off. Be careful to close your car windows at the entry gates and at Baboon Cliff in case you encounter any baboons and monkeys. Note also that approaching the shoreline on foot is discouraged.

THE BIRDING

If you enter from the Main Gate, you quickly reach the road that goes around the lake. The nearby camp site on your right and the woodland along the road are among the best places in the country to look for the uncommon **Grey-crested Helmetshrike**. Also look here for the more common **White-crested Helmetshrike**, as well as **Coqui Francolin**, **Blue-spotted Wood Dove** (uncommon), **Pearl-spotted Owlet**, **Arrow-marked Babbler** and **Rüppell's Starling**.

Grey-crested Helmetshrike

A left turn past a bridge over the Njoro River offers the first of many stunning vistas of hundreds of thousands of **Lesser Flamingo**, often seen wading with **Black-winged Stilt** and **Pied Avocet**. The fresh water at the Njoro mouth attracts **African Spoonbill**, **Great White Pelican**, **Grey-headed Gull** and sometimes **Western Reef Heron** and **Dimorphic Egret**. Scan the trees as your approach the river mouth for **African Fish Eagle** and, in season, October–March, **Steppe** and **Greater Spotted eagles**, although some remain in the area throughout the year.

At the shoreline there may be herons, ibises, **Ringed** (in season) and **Kittlitz's plovers** and, also in season, **Marsh**, **Green**, **Wood**, **Common** and **Curlew** sandpipers, as well as **Little** and **Temminck's stints** and **Ruff**. Look in the water for rafts of **Black-necked Grebe** and possibly a **Great Crested Grebe**. Flocks of **Gull-billed**, **Whiskered** and **White-winged Black** terns may number in the thousands.

African Spoonbill

Drive up to Baboon Cliff to enjoy spectacular views. Also note **Cliff Chat** on boulders in the vicinity and watch **Nyanza Swift** crisscross in the void below. Overhead there may be **Grey-rumped** and **Mosque swallows**, migrant harriers and eagles.

Various types of accommodation are available in Nakuru town. Keep in mind that once you exit you will have to purchase new tickets to re-enter the park. Within the park there are the Wildlife Clubs of Kenya Hostel (www.wildlifeclubsofkenya.org), many camp sites and some more luxurious facilities, including Lion Hill Lodge (www.sarovahotels.com/lionhill-nakuru/) and Lake Nakuru Lodge (www.lakenakurulodge.com/).

If you decide to leave the circuit road and explore the southern portion of the park, you may spot the increasingly rare **Southern Ground Hornbill**. At Makalia Waterfalls **Slender-billed Starling** dip into the water. On your way there, look out for **Horus Swift**, **Plain Martin**, **White-fronted Bee-eater** and **Abyssinian Wheatear**, all of which breed in the calcite earth cliffs.

As you drive to rejoin the road around the lake, check the freshwater pools at Muya's Causeway for waders and ducks, including **Cape Teal**. If you are staying at the Lion Hill Lodge, look there for **Hildebrandt's Francolin** and **Little Rock Thrush**.

In the woodlands on the northern shore there may be **Black Cuckoo**, **Verreaux's Eagle Owl**, **Broad-billed Roller**, **Striped Kingfisher**, **Common Scimitarbill**, **Scaly-throated Honeyguide**, **Red-throated Wryneck**, **Nubian Woodpecker**, **Northern Puffback**, **Red-faced Crombec** and **African Thrush**.

To access the shore here, try the track to Hippo Point (often muddy after rains), which is a lakeside viewpoint beside a freshwater stream, along which you may find **Black-tailed Godwit** and **Spotted Redshank**.

OTHER WILDLIFE

A great deal of game is managed in this park, including large numbers of buffalo and some of the highest concentrations of black and white rhinos in the country.

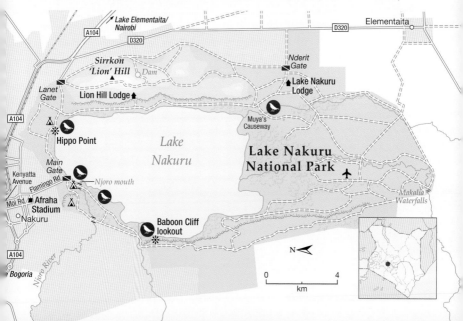

LAKE BOGORIA IBA

KEY SPECIES
Black-necked Grebe, Lesser Flamingo, Greater Flamingo, Cape Teal, Lesser Kestrel, Pallid Harrier, Silverbird.

The most saline and alkaline of Kenya's Rift Valley lakes, Bogoria is perhaps also the most dramatic. The Siracho Escarpment rises abruptly from the lake's eastern shore, while spectacular hot springs and steam geysers are clustered on the flatter western shoreline and in the south. This 107km² reserve is a major feeding ground for hundreds of thousands of **Lesser Flamingo**. They come to feed on the blue-green algae *Spirulina,* which sometimes gives the lake a greenish colour.

A hot spring at Lake Bogoria

HABITAT
The thick bush to the west of Bogoria is dominated by *Acacia-Commiphora* bush and desert date *Balanites aegyptica*. Close to the western shoreline the naked branches of submerged trees may jut out above the fluctuating waters. The lake is fed by hot springs, the Waseges River in the north and the seasonal Emos and Mugun rivers in the southwest, but has no outlet, losing water mostly by evaporation. Riverside trees include large figs and *Acacia tortilis.* Some salt-resistant grasses cover the rocky lava soils, like those at the hot springs.

Lesser Flamingos never breed at Lake Bogoria.

Approach the springs with caution, as there are few barriers and the ground can be uneven, rocky and slippery.

GETTING THERE

From Nakuru take the Nakuru–Sigor Road (B4). (See also Site 28 Lake Baringo.) To reach Loboi Gate, the main entry into Lake Bogoria National Reserve, turn right 3.5km before Marigat town, at the signposted turn-off for Lake Bogoria. Loboi Gate is 19km down this road.

VISITOR INFO

The single main track that used to go right around the lake has only survived along the western and southern shorelines, and even here it has been greatly reduced because of recent persistently high water levels. Ask at the gate for information about the state of the track, as some attempts have been made to reconnect it, with newer sections replacing the older ones that have been submerged.

The lake has been a national reserve since 1973, and both entry and camping fees are levied. Rudimentary camping is the only option for overnight accommodation in the reserve, although the best-positioned camp sites, Acacia, Riverside and (perhaps best of all) Fig Tree in the south, are currently under water or inaccessible. The Lake Bogoria Spa Resort (www.facebook.com/lakebogoriaspa) and various budget accommodation options are found outside the reserve, close to Loboi Gate.

THE BIRDING

Lake Bogoria may host congregations of more than a million **Lesser Flamingo**, especially when the algae die back at Lake Nakuru (Site 26). It is a truly impressive spectacle, and the loud 'honking' a sound that one recalls for years. Look among the flamingos for **Cape Teal**, **Little Grebe**, **Greater Flamingo**, **African Spoonbill**, **Great White Pelican** and **Red-knobbed Coot**. Lake Bogoria is the best place in the country to see **Black-necked Grebe**, and often a few thousand may be seen way out in the middle of the lake. They rarely, if ever, come close to shore.

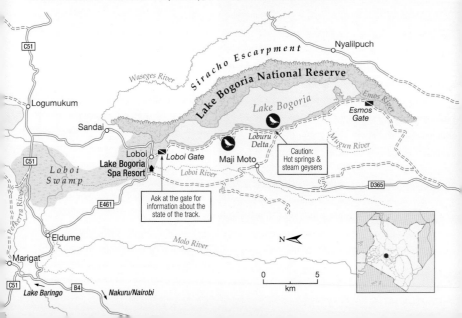

Pallid Harriers migrate through the country between October and April.

The track from Loboi Gate down along the western shore of the lake passes through thick bush and emerges at intervals onto the exposed shore, for instance at Loboru Delta, which is popular for its active geysers. (Although, when the water level is high, the geysers are submerged.) **Black-winged Stilt**, **Pied Avocet** and **Spur-winged**, **Kittlitz's** and **Three-banded plovers** are common along the lake's margins. Also look for **Black-tailed Godwit**, **Common Greenshank** and **Wood** and **Common sandpipers**. Migrant visitors seen in season, October–April, include the **White-winged Black** and **Gull-billed terns**, as well as **Lesser Kestrel**, **Pallid Harrier** and **Steppe Eagle**.

It gets exceptionally hot here, and the trees near the shore offer some welcome relief. They are also good for **Rufous-crowned Roller**, **Red-billed Hornbill**, **Rüppell's Starling**, **Silverbird** and **Grosbeak Canary**.

On the landward side of the track is dense dry bush where **Grey-headed** and **Woodland kingfishers**, **Green Wood-hoopoe**, **Nubian Woodpecker**, **Chestnut-headed Sparrow Lark** and **Eastern Violet-backed** and **Beautiful sunbirds** occur. Other birds found here include the **Yellow-spotted Petronia** and the **Speckle-fronted**, **Lesser Masked** and stunning **Red-headed weavers**.

OTHER WILDLIFE

The immediate surroundings of the lake are the best place in Kenya to see the magnificent greater kudu, which has large spiralling horns. However, it is very shy and tends to stay on the far side of the lake, so you will need binoculars.

Except at the coast and in the driest of northern areas, the Red-headed Weaver is found widely.

LAKE BARINGO IBA

KEY SPECIES
Allen's Gallinule, Northern White-faced Scops Owl, Hemprich's Hornbill, Jackson's Hornbill, Pygmy Batis, Red-fronted Warbler, Bristle-crowned Starling, Brown-tailed Rock Chat, White-billed Buffalo-Weaver, Little Weaver, Northern Masked Weaver, Northern Red Bishop.

Situated between the Laikipia Plateau in the east and the Tugen Hills in the west, Baringo is a shallow lake with no outlet. Only a small part of the lake in the west has been developed for visitors. Nonetheless, the lake, its islands and the lava cliffs on its western shore are a birder's paradise, with a list exceeding 500 species, some of which are highly localized.

HABITAT
Fed by a number of rivers, the 168km² Lake Baringo is one of only two substantial freshwater basins on the floor of the Rift Valley in Kenya. Many of the acacia trees growing on its shore have been inundated by an unprecedented and unexplained recent rise in the lake's water levels. Other plants that occur here include the toothbrush tree, also known as 'mswaki', *Salvadora persica*, *Delonix elata*, *Balanites* and *Terminalia brownii*, as well as the beautiful desert rose *Adenium obesum*. The area is hot and semi-arid, and although there is some farming, the people are mainly pastoralists.

GETTING THERE
From Nakuru take the Nakuru–Sigor Road (B4) in a northerly direction and continue straight to Marigat (about 96km from Nakuru). Drive through Marigat, crossing the *luggas*, which may be full after good rains, and, after about 15km, turn right onto the shore road towards Kampi-ya-Samaki.

Once you have settled into your accommodation, head for the grand basalt cliffs west of the lake to start birding.

You will need to return to the junction on the B4 where you turned right towards Kampi-ya-Samaki, and instead head north for 2km, turning left at the sign that reads 'Kaposi Birds Watching'. Drive for 100m along this track to a parking area.

VISITOR INFO
The Lake Baringo conservation area now charges a small access fee. If you're looking for overnight accommodation, the budget-friendly Roberts Camp (robertscamp.com) on the southwestern shore has survived the high water levels and is a favourite with birders. Other facilities are available nearby and on the lake's islands. Boat rides can be arranged directly with the various camps and lodges. Plan to do your birding in the early mornings and late afternoons, to avoid the heat of the day.

The grand cliffs west of Lake Baringo are a good place to look for birds of prey.

The cryptic plumage of Heuglin's Courser makes it hard to find during the day.

Peter Steward

THE BIRDING

The basalt cliffs are commanded by the very large and incredibly beautiful **Verreaux's Eagle** and are also home to some of the 'specials' of northwestern Kenya – **Hemprich's Hornbill**, **Fan-tailed Raven** and **Bristle-crowned Starling**. Look among the boulders at the base of the cliffs for **Brown-tailed Rock Chat** (another special of the area) and **Mocking Cliff Chat**.

Weave your way slowly back to the parking or road. As you go, search the dry scrub for **Jacobin** and **Diederik cuckoos**, **Red-fronted Barbet**, **Pygmy Batis**, **Sulphur-breasted Bushshrike**, **Three-streaked Tchagra**, **Brubru**, **Mouse-coloured Penduline Tit**, **Red-fronted Warbler** and, in mixed flocks, numerous *Estrildidae* spp. **Lanner Falcon**, **Dark Chanting Goshawk** and **Spotted Eagle Owl** frequent the area below the cliffs as well.

Northern Red Bishop

Jacques Pitteloud

Away from the cliffs, on the opposite side of the B4, there are grassy rocky plains with scattered bushes. In season (October–April) this can be a good area in which to find **Great Spotted Cuckoo**, **Rufous Bush Chat**, **Common Rock Thrush** and various migrant wheatears and shrikes. Look out for **Spotted Thick-knee**, the very dapper **Heuglin's Courser** and **Lichtenstein's Sandgrouse** in the shade under the bushes. **Slender-tailed Nightjar** may also be well camouflaged on the ground. After good rains **Yellow-crowned** and **Northern Red Bishop** occur here too.

The shore teems with birds, many of them tame and confiding. **White-bellied Go-away-bird** comes down to the ground to pick fruit, and the highly localized **Jackson's Hornbill** is common. Weavers on view include **Little**, **Village** and **Golden-backed weavers**, as well as a disjunct population of the **Northern Masked Weaver**, a species found at Lake Baringo and in the Omo Delta at Lake Turkana and nowhere else in Kenya. **White-billed Buffalo-Weaver** breed in huge noisy colonies in some of the taller trees. **African Scops Owl** and **Northern White-faced Scops Owl** are often found roosting at or near camp sites. Local guides are excellent at finding the special birds of the area.

Peter Usher

Northern White-faced Scops Owl

The water birds seen from shore or by way of a boat excursion may include many herons, **Great White Egret** and, where there are reeds, the rare **Allen's Gallinule**. Feeding **African Fish Eagles** is a popular activity on boat trips.

OTHER WILDLIFE

Seven fish species occur in the lake, including an endemic tilapia *Oreochromis niloticus baringoensis*. Local Njemp fishermen paddling in their low, flat balsa boats are a familiar site on the lake. Watch out for crocodile and hippo that come out to feed on the grassy banks around the lake. Reptiles and amphibians also thrive here.

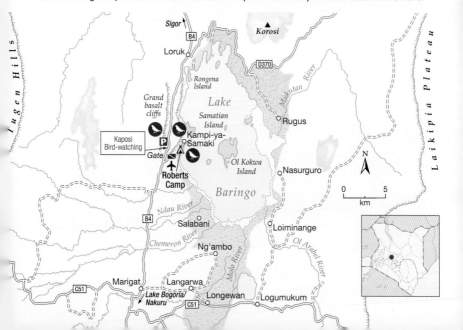

SOUTHERN KERIO VALLEY

KEY SPECIES

Dark Chanting Goshawk, Four-banded Sandgrouse, White-crested Turaco, Hemprich's Hornbill, Jackson's Hornbill, White-crested Helmetshrike, Fan-tailed Raven, Ethiopian Swallow, Chestnut-crowned Sparrow Weaver, Familiar Chat, Gambaga Flycatcher, Red-fronted Warbler. **Passage migrants:** Common Rock Thrush.

Kerio Valley in northwestern Kenya is a branch of the Great Rift Valley. It is a patchwork of homesteads and farms, traversed by streams that flow into the Kerio River. It forms part of the range of the **Four-banded Sandgrouse** and of **Jackson's Hornbill** and is a 'flyway' – part of a route regularly used by large numbers of migratory birds.

HABITAT

The drive down into the valley offers stunning views of the Keiyo-Marakwet Escarpment, with its steep-sided forested slopes, and of Lake Kamnarok in the distance. (In recent years this lake has frequently dried up.) The valley, which lies at an altitude of 1,132m, is semi-arid and much of it is under cultivation, irrigated largely in the traditional way, using water furrows. The natural vegetation comprises mostly *Acacia-Commiphora* scrub, with *Sansevieria* thickets and a scattering of aloes and desert rose *Adenium obesum*. *Terminalia brownii* is found throughout the valley.

GETTING THERE

Take the C51 out of Eldoret and stay on this road all the way to Iten town – Kenya's 'Home of Champions'. Iten lies at a height of 2,346m, near the edge of the escarpment, and is known for the number of Kenyan marathon winners that hail from here. From Iten, take the winding road down past the Torok waterfalls and the Tambach Centre to the little village of Biretwo, where you will turn onto the C52 road leading to Tot. This is currently a poor dirt road and poses a real challenge, even with a four-wheel drive. Carry on as far as you can, stopping for birds along the way.

Bush and acacia woodland in the Kerio Valley

It is also possible to reach Biretwo from the east via Kabarnet, if you are travelling from Lake Bogoria or Lake Baringo (Sites 27 and 28).

VISITOR INFO

The area is extensive, but the challenging road conditions may limit the distance you can go, so it is best planned as a day excursion. Skirt the small farms when exploring on foot. If you end up leaving your car for a significant length of time, you may find homesteaders eager to assure you of how carefully they have watched your car, in expectation of a small gratuity. The nearest visitor facilities if you are approaching from the west are at Iten, where the few hotels and guest houses have great views of the valley. The Kerio Valley has become a popular paragliding spot.

THE BIRDING

As you begin your descent into the valley, watch out for **Hemprich's Hornbill** in the trees that grow between rocks on the cliffs, as well as for **Ross's Turaco** flying through the woodlands on the lower slopes of the escarpment, and for **Fan-tailed Raven** rising on the thermals.

Drive along slowly and park offroad to bird-watch wherever you see interesting birds. Resident birds around the homesteads abutting the road include **Speckled Pigeon, Hoopoe, Green Wood-hoopoe, D'Arnaud's Barbet, Black-headed Batis** (uncommon), **Northern Puffback, Superb** and **Rüppell's Long-tailed starlings, African Paradise**

Peter Usher

Rüppell's Long-tailed Starling

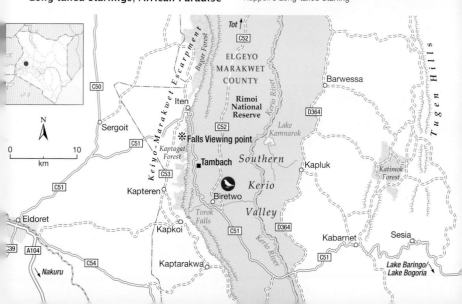

Black-headed Oriole

Red-fronted Warbler

White-crested Turaco

Flycatcher (white morph), **African Yellow White-eye** and sunbirds (including **Amethyst, Hunter's, Marico** and **Beautiful**).

Explore patches of thorn trees away from the road for **Diederik Cuckoo**, groups of striking **White-crested Helmetshrike, Sulphur-breasted Bushshrike**, the eye-catching **Black-headed Gonolek, Black-headed Oriole, Northern Brownbul**, the northern race of **Red-fronted Warbler, Red-winged Starling** and the dazzling **Violet-backed Starling** (an Afrotropic migrant). Also keep an eye out for **Jackson's Hornbill**, which is common only here, in the northwest of the country.

Four-banded Sandgrouse, Chestnut-crowned Sparrow Weaver and groups of **Familiar Chat** (which has red on its rump and the sides of the tail), waxbills and buntings may be foraging on the ground in open scrub and rocky areas.

Back on the road, **White-fronted Bee-eater** may be hawking for insects from nearby scrub and trees, which may also produce **Boran Cisticola, Pale** and **Gambaga flycatchers** and **Reichenow's Seedeater**. From October to April **Spotted Flycatcher** may be common and **Great Spotted Cuckoo, Eastern Olivaceous Warbler** and **Common Rock Thrush** can occur almost anywhere. Along with the odd paraglider, there may be **Bateleur** and **Wahlberg's Eagle** in the skies above.

Other birds typical of the Kerio Valley are **Emerald-spotted Wood Dove, White-bellied Go-away-bird, Pearl-spotted Owlet, Rufous-crowned Roller, African Black, Mottled** and **Nyanza swifts, Ethiopian Swallow, Crowned** and **African Grey hornbills, Brown-crowned Tchagra, Northern White-crowned Shrike, Brown Babbler**, barbets, honeyguides and woodpeckers.

Large sycamore figs *Ficus sycamorus* provide shade along streams as well as fruit for birds and are often good for **Meyer's Parrot, Black Cuckooshrike** and the amazingly beautiful **White-crested Turaco**.

OTHER WILDLIFE

In addition to vervet monkey, baboon, bush squirrel, butterflies, other insects and reptiles, there are remnant populations of elephant and buffalo in the Kerio Valley. The Rimoi National Reserve, with an area of just 66km², has been restocked and reopened, but is best approached from a different direction.

SITE 30

KAKAMEGA FOREST [IBA]

KEY SPECIES

Western Banded Snake Eagle, African Crowned Eagle, White-spotted Flufftail, Grey Parrot, Great Blue Turaco, Blue-headed Bee-eater, Yellow-billed Barbet, Ansorge's Greenbul, Toro Olive Greenbul, Southern Hyliota, Turner's Eremomela, Grey-chested Illadopsis, Chapin's Flycatcher.

Kakamega Forest is a 'must do' site for birders. It is the only remnant of Guineo-Congolese rainforest in Kenya and therefore much of its flora and fauna are found nowhere else in the country. Special birds include **Blue-headed Bee-eater**, **Chapin's Flycatcher** and **Turner's Eremomela**, which are found only here and at the nearby South Nandi Forest. In addition to these species, and despite the challenges of birding under a dense canopy, you can anticipate a good-sized bird list including barbets, greenbuls, illadopses, flycatchers, shrikes and the **Great Blue Turaco**.

HABITAT

Kenya Wildlife Service administers Kakamega Forest National Reserve (44km²) in the north, while the rest falls under the Kenya Forest Service. In area it totals 240km², and the vegetation consists of shrubs, lianas and more than 120 forest tree species, such as stinkwood *Celtis mildbraedii*, *Aningeria altissima*, Elgon teak *Olea capensis* subsp. *welwitschii*, *Croton* spp. and *Maesopsis eminii*. One *Maesopsis eminii*, called Mama Mutere, is said to have been 300 years old when it finally fell in 2013.

There are also rivers, the Yala and Isiukhu, streams and a mosaic of open glades, ponds and guava, tea and tree plantations.

GETTING THERE

Take the A104 from Nakuru and drive for about 95km to Timboroa. Continue past Timboroa for 10km, then turn left onto the C36 and continue for another 48km to Kapsabet via Lessos. You will cross the equator on the way.

Alternatively, start from Eldoret town and go southwest on the C39 for about 46km to Kapsabet. Continue through Kapsabet and drive for 19km on the Stendi Kisa–Yala Road (C39), turning right just after Chepsonoi Market onto a murram road signposted 'St. Anne's Ikuywa Sec. Sch.' and 'Rondo Retreat 9.7km'. Continue for 14km until you reach the Isecheno Forest Station.

To access the forest from the west, travel north on the A1 from Kisumu to Kakamega. Just north of Chavakali, pass the junction for the C39 to Kapsabet and continue for another 11km. Turn right at Khayega (before the post office on your left and the National Oil filling station on your

Birders at Kakamega Forest

right) and drive for 12km along the rough road past Shinyalu Market to the forest station. From this point, Rondo Retreat is another 2.5km drive. For a smoother ride, don't turn right at Khayega. Instead, continue until Mukumu High School is on your left. Turn right here, drive for about 6km, looping around on the Mukumu–Lirhanda Road to a junction, then turn right to Shinyalu Market and proceed as above.

VISITOR INFO

The wettest months are April to August, although it rains year-round. While bird-watching along the murram roads be vigilant – nowadays cars and motorcycle taxis (boda bodas) use these roads as alternative routes to reach villages and towns on the periphery of the forest.

If you wish to overnight near the forest you have a few options. There are four double rooms at the Forest

THE BIRDING

The road that runs from the forest barrier, passes Rondo Retreat and leads to the Ikuywa River creates a 'clearing' that makes observation easier, despite the intermittent traffic. Start out early to find starlings and **Grey Parrot**, which may stop on top of the tallest trees to catch the first rays of sun. **Mackinnon's Shrike**, **African Blue** and **Dusky Crested flycatchers** and **African Thrush** are common (characteristically western) species that are also likely to be about.

Examine the scrub and yellow-flowered *Tithonia* on the roadside for **Banded** and **White-chinned prinia**, **Black-throated** and **Buff-throated apalis**, **Olive-green Camaroptera** and **Black-faced Rufous Warbler**. Movement behind the scrub and in the lower tree canopy may alert you to **Jameson's Wattle-eye**, **Lühder's Bushshrike**, **Northern Double-collared Sunbird** or the **Green-headed Sunbird**.

Finding and working out skulking greenbuls is rather more vexing than you'd believe from their constant chatter – **Yellow-whiskered**, **Slender-billed** and **Joyful greenbuls** are more common than the **Shelley's**, **Little**, rare **Little Grey**, **Ansorge's** and **Toro Olive greenbuls**, which are more likely in the lower tree canopy. The raucous call of **Black-and-white Casqued Hornbill** can be a welcome distraction. These are large birds, which, along with the amazing **Great Blue Turaco**, are hard to overlook.

As you walk, scan the road ahead of you. Above the forest there may be **Western Banded Snake Eagle**, while **White-tailed Ant Thrush** may be found on the road ahead, and, sweeping back and forth in large numbers, there could be **White-headed Saw-wing**, **Barn** (in season) and **Mosque swallows**.

Other typical residents include **African Emerald Cuckoo**, **Yellowbill**, **Brown-eared Woodpecker**, **Pink-footed Puffback**, **Petit's Cuckooshrike**, **Yellow-throated Leaflove**, **Uganda Woodland Warbler**, **Southern Hyliota**, **Turner's Eremomela** (endangered), **Black-billed**, **Vieillot's Black** and

Shelley's Greenbul

Peter Usher

Rest House, a raised wooden building facing the forest. You can also camp on the grounds there or make use of nearby community bandas. The house and bandas are basic and self-catering and are located near the Isecheno Forest Station. You can arrange to get local food prepared for you. Alternatively, you could stay in more comfort at Rondo (www.rondoretreat.com), a charming Christian retreat, 4km from the forest station, with gardens in the forest itself. Contact them at rondo@trinityfellowship.or.ke.

In the forest birds can often only be heard, and you will vastly increase your chances of identifying the species you hear by hiring a local guide. Enquire at the Isecheno Forest Station or at Rondo for guides. If you go birding in the forest station area, you'll be expected to pay a visitors' fee.

Blue-headed Bee-eater

Brown-capped weavers, **Red-headed Malimbe**, **Grey-headed Negrofinch** and **Oriole Finch**.

A signpost that reads 'River Yala Nature Trail 3HRS Walking' leads down a narrow, sometimes muddy, track just beyond Rondo. Check the canopy of tall trees closing in over you here for the rare **Chapin's Flycatcher**. Sitting quietly lower down in the canopy there may be **Bar-tailed Trogon** and low in the undergrowth nearer the river there may be **Grey-chested Illadopsis** and **Blue-shouldered** and **Snowy-headed robin chats**. The gorgeous **Blue-headed Bee-eater** is sometimes seen on the road, but is a regular at the river.

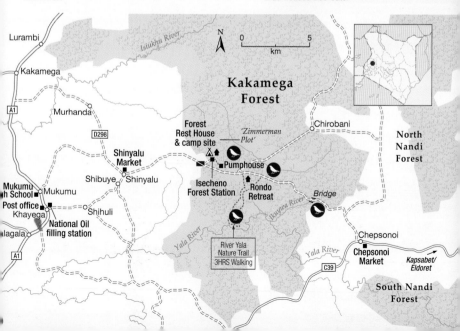

Ross's Turaco shows stunning red flight feathers in flight.

Another good birding trail off this road can be found by driving to the Ikuywa River. The trail is on the right soon after crossing the bridge.

Rondo Retreat's beautiful garden is a great place to find numerous species, among them **White-headed Wood-hoopoe** and **Grey-throated**, **Double-toothed**, and **Yellow-billed barbets**. An African Crowned Eagle has nested in a tree in front of the dining hall, while **Ross's Turaco** is a frequent visitor. With some perseverance you can find **White-spotted Flufftail** and the equally shy **Equatorial Akalat** near the fish ponds located in the lower garden.

Near to the forest station there are several paths and trails referred to as the 'Zimmerman Plot' (named after ornithologist and illustrator Dale Zimmerman), as well as a track to the pumphouse. These are worth exploring for alethes and illadopses, including the more vocal **Scaly-breasted Illadopsis,** which feeds on the forest floor.

Black-and-white Casqued Hornbill

OTHER WILDLIFE

This forest is a thriving ecosystem with hundreds of plant and animal species. This is probably the best place to see red-tailed monkey and giant forest squirrel. Also conspicuous are colobus and blue monkeys and baboon. There are bushbuck, beetles, moths, dragonflies, over 400 butterfly and 61 reptile species, including many snakes, some of which, like the Gabon viper, Jameson's mamba and rhinoceros viper, are characteristic of Guineo-Congolese rainforest.

SOUTH NANDI FOREST IBA

KEY SPECIES

Great Blue Turaco, Bar-tailed Trogon, Blue-headed Bee-eater, Least Honeyguide, Petit's Cuckooshrike, Shelley's Greenbul, Southern Hyliota, Uganda Woodland Warbler, Turner's Eremomela, Grey-chested Babbler, Equatorial Akalat, Chapin's Flycatcher. **Passage migrants:** Steppe Buzzard, Eurasian Bee-eater.

South Nandi Forest is one of the best places to see the endangered **Turner's Eremomela**, which is locally common. **Chapin's Flycatcher** is also widespread along the forest edge, but occurs in smaller numbers. Both species frequent the southern part of the forest, known as the Kobujoi Block. It is the largest of the administrative blocks of South Nandi Forest – an area of about 17,960ha, lying at an altitude of 1,700m.

HABITAT

A walk in the Kobujoi Block will take you through forest consisting predominantly of *Croton megalocarpus*, which grow very tall here, *Strombosia schefferi* and *Tabernaemontana stapfiana*. The area receives regular rainfall, which makes for thick mossy undergrowth and muddy tracks.

GETTING THERE

Kobujoi is about 40km from Kapsabet by way of the Nandi Hills–Kapsabet and Kipsigak–Serem roads. At Kobujoi turn right onto the almost parallel Kobujoi–Chepkumia Road and drive for 1.5km, passing Chebisaas Girls' School, to reach the Kobujoi Forest Station.

An alternative approach is from the Kisumu–Kakamega (A1) road. At Chavakali, exit onto the C39 road to Kapsabet and Eldoret and head for the Shamakhokho Trading Centre. At the town centre (a busy bus-stop area) turn right and take the Kipsigak–Serem Road for 20km, passing through Serem to reach Kobujoi.

VISITOR INFO

There is a visitor centre at the Kobujoi Forest Station, where you can obtain the services of a guide and information on forest trails. Close to the station there are two bandas, each consisting of two rooms and a bathroom. There is also a camping area, but no kitchen facilities. Limited accommodation is available in the town of Kobujoi. About 34km away, in Nandi Hill town, there is The Tea Planter's Inn, which can be found on Facebook. For a local bird guide, email office@naturekenya.org.

Tea estates flourish in the Nandi Hills.

Turner's Eremomela

THE BIRDING

Birds encountered in the clearings around the forest station include **Yellow-rumped Tinkerbird, Lesser Honeyguide, Hairy-breasted Barbet, Black-throated** and **Grey apalis, African Yellow White-eye, Chapin's** and **African Dusky flycatchers, Chubb's Cisticola** and **Green-headed, Scarlet-chested** and **Northern Double-collared sunbirds**.

Vieillot's Black Weaver

From the forest station you can walk or drive down the main all-weather forest road. On one side of the road the vegetation is kept clear and is restricted to low trees and scrub, as a power line runs parallel to the road. Look out for flocks of **Blue-headed, Cinnamon-chested** and (in season) **Eurasian bee-eaters** hawking for insects from the wires, **Vieillot's Black Weaver, Chin-spot Batis** and **Dusky Tit** moving about in the tree canopy, **Grey-chested Babbler** and **Brown-chested Alethe** skulking around in the lower boughs and **Thick-billed Seedeater** foraging for fruit in the bushes. Scan above the band of road running away from you for **African Goshawk, Steppe Buzzard** (in season, October–April), **Long-crested Eagle** and **Crowned Eagle**, all of which use the road to scout for prey. Also flying between the trees there may be swallows, including the **Black Saw-wing** and **Barn swallows** (in season), while the arrival of **Great Blue Turaco** can hardly go unnoticed.

About 1.5km after the forest station there is a smaller, less disturbed track that branches left. Explore the understorey and canopy of the denser forest along this track. Birds of interest here include **Bar-tailed Trogon, Least Honeyguide** (uncommon), **Pink-footed Puffback, Petit's Cuckooshrike, Shelley's, Plain, Slender-billed, Joyful** and **Cabanis's greenbuls, Southern Hyliota, Uganda Woodland Warbler, Turner's Eremomela, Stuhlmann's** and **Sharpe's starlings, Equatorial Akalat, Blue-shouldered Robin Chat, Black-billed** and **Brown-capped weavers, Red-headed Malimbe, Grey-headed Negrofinch** and **Oriole Finch**.

OTHER WILDLIFE

You will be alerted to the presence of monkeys by their calls. Species found here include black-and-white colobus, blue, red-tailed and, if you're lucky, De Brazza's monkeys. The red-legged sun squirrel is also quite active, and, very rarely, the secretive golden cat is spotted.

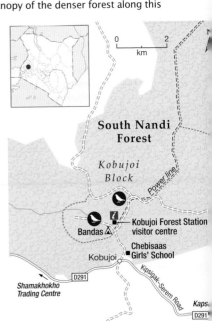

South Nandi Forest

Kobujoi Block

Power line

Kobujoi Forest Station visitor centre

Bandas

Chebisaas Girls' School

Kobujoi

D291

Shamakhokho Trading Centre

Kipsigak-Serem Road

Kaps.

D291

MASAI MARA NATIONAL RESERVE IBA

KEY SPECIES

Red-necked Spurfowl, Rufous-bellied Heron, Western Banded Snake Eagle, Ovambo Sparrowhawk, Schalow's Turaco, Bare-faced Go-away-bird, D'Arnaud's Barbet (Usambiro Barbet), Southern Ground Hornbill, Golden-tailed Woodpecker, Magpie Shrike, Trilling Cisticola, Rock-loving Cisticola, Long-tailed Cisticola, Karamoja Apalis, Pale Wren Warbler, Yellow-bellied Hyliota, Green-capped Eremomela, Yellow-billed Oxpecker, Familiar Chat, Northern Black Flycatcher, Rufous-tailed Weaver

This is the reserve of *Out of Africa* and *Big Cat Diary* fame. It is renowned for its annual game migration, one of the most incredible sights in nature. Its birdlife is equally spectacular, with over 550 species recorded in the Mara, among them **Rufous-bellied Heron**, **Ovambo Sparrowhawk**, **Schalow's Turaco** and **Magpie Shrike**, which are consistently seen in few other places.

HABITAT

The Mara measures 1,510km². Its glowing savanna stretches from the Loita Hills in the east to the Oloololo Escarpment (altitude 1,829m) in the west. The Mara River flows from the northeast, traverses the park and exits in the south. The area between the river and the escarpment in the west is known as the Mara Triangle.

Other rivers that flow through the Mara include the Talek in the northeast and the Sand River in the southeast.

The grassland is scattered with *Boscia coriacea* and *Balanites*, and alternates with wooded watercourses and *Acacia* bush thickets. The riverine woodlands include East African greenheart *Diospyros abyssinica*, small-fruited teclea *Vepris nobilis*, diamond-leaved euclea *Euclea divinorum* and figs *Ficus* spp. The thickets in the east have many orange-and-green-leafed *Croton dichogamus* and scented leleshwa *Tarchonanthus camphoratus* bushes, while on the escarpment there are remnants of western highland forest.

This track ascends the Oloololo Escarpment from the Mara Plains.

Female Coqui Francolin

GETTING THERE

Note that owing to the vast size of the area not all of the route described below is shown on the map opposite. To Mara's Sekenani Gate from Narok town, get onto the Narok–Sotik (B3) road and drive for about 4km until you reach a well-signposted junction to Sekenani Gate. Turn left onto the C12 and continue for 12km. The road bears left soon after crossing the Ewaso Ny'iro River and continues to the southeast. The trip from Narok to the gate is a distance of 86km in total. Note that the road is very rough and it is slow going.

To reach the Oloololo Gate from Narok town, you will also get onto the Narok–Sotik (B3) road, but this time pass the signposted junction to Sekenani Gate and continue for 28km, before turning left and travelling on the C13 through Ngorengore and Lemek, passing straight through (in a southwesterly direction) the crossroads about 14km from the B3 junction and on via the small centres of Aitong and Mara Rianta to the gate. It's a total of 110km. Some of this route goes through the Mara North Conservancy, is on badly corrugated road, and is difficult to pass in places when wet.

To reach the Oloololo Escarpment and Saparingo Valley, exit the Mara Triangle from Oloololo Gate and drive for about 1km to reach the first of two tracks to the left before the Kichwa Tembo turn-off on the right. The first is a continuation of the C13 as described above and takes you up the escarpment. The second, after another 1km, also takes you up the escarpment by way of the Saparingo Valley and the Saparingo stream.

VISITOR INFO

This very popular park can get crowded during the months of the great migration (July–September). The camps and lodges in and around the reserve may be at full capacity, and there will be many more vehicles than usual – important considerations in deciding when to visit and where to stay.

The larger part of the reserve is managed by Narok County, while the 510km^2 Mara Triangle is managed by the Mara Conservancy together with Trans-Mara County. Around the reserve there are other Maasai community wildlife conservancies. It is preferable to pay for entry on the side of the park where you will be staying. However, on each side you can get a two-hour free transit voucher, allowing you to cross over. A ticket is valid for 24 hours. Visit **maratriangle.org/visit/conservation-fees/** for the latest fees.

Levaillant's Cuckoo, an uncommon Afrotropic migrant, seen May–September

THE BIRDING

■ *Mara grasslands:* The grasslands of the Mara are as rich in birdlife as they are in mammals. Watch resting buffalo or grazing rhino for **Red-billed** or **Yellow-billed** oxpeckers, and check around the feet of grazing elephants for **Cattle Egret** catching insects. **Common Buzzards** in season (October–April) or a committee of critically endangered **White-backed Vulture** may sit atop a lone *Balanites* tree. In season, look out for the thousands of **Eurasian Bee-eater** and **Barn Swallow** that may pass through; also scan the air over marshes for **Common Swift** and **Sand Martin**. **Rattling Cisticola** may be singing at every turn. Other species of cisticola found in the Mara include the **Red-faced**, **Winding**, **Stout**, **Croaking**, **Siffling**, **Long-tailed**, **Zitting**, **Desert**, **Black-backed** and **Pectoral-patch cisticolas**.

Game birds like **Coqui** and **Hildebrandt's francolins** and Red-necked Spurfowl are easier to identify. They may be seen on the tracks, but generally try to stay out of sight of the keen-eyed raptors hunting from above, which can range from the tiny

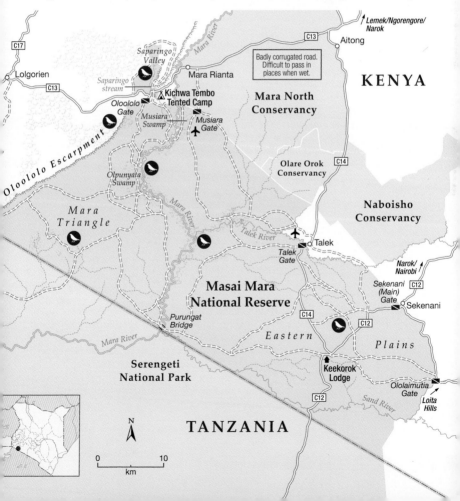

Peter Usher

Grey-headed Bushshrike

Pygmy Falcon to large eagles such as **Western Banded Snake Eagle**, as well as **African Marsh Harrier**, **African Goshawk**, **Lizard Buzzard**, **Booted Eagle** and, in season, **Lesser Kestrel** and **Eleonora's** and **Sooty** falcons.

Other grassland birds include **Black-bellied Bustard**, **Crowned**, **African Wattled** and (in season) **Caspian plovers**, **Temminck's** and **Double-banded coursers**, sandgrouse, **White-tailed**, **Flappet** and **Fawn-coloured larks**, numerous **Grey-headed** (Swahili) **Sparrow**, colourful **Yellow-throated** and **Rosy-breasted longclaws**, **Jackson's Widowbird** and **Grassland Pipit.**

Pairs of **Karamoja Apalis** and the uncommon **Magpie Shrike** are found only in the eastern valleys and plains, which receive less rain than those in the west. The large **Southern Ground Hornbill**, typically seen walking in the grass, is found in the eastern Mara. **Bare-faced Go-Away Bird** is yet another uncommon bird regularly seen in the east. Look among the thickets in the east and southeast for a good variety of bush birds including a great many cuckoos, **Grey-headed** and **Sulphur-breasted bushshrikes**, **Red-throated Tit**, **Grey Penduline Tit**, **Capped Wheatear**, **Common Whitethroat** (in season) and **Speckle-fronted**, **Little** and **Parasitic weavers**. **Rufous-tailed Weaver** now breeds in the Mara.

■ *Woodlands and wetlands:* The woodlands of the Mara River are favoured by flycatchers (like the **African Blue** and **Ashy** flycatchers), honeyguides and **Green-backed woodpeckers**, as well as **Golden-tailed Woodpecker**, which is also seen in the remnant woodlands on the Mombasa Road (see Site 46). The **Violet-backed Starling**, a stunning Afrotropic migrant, is a not infrequent visitor. **Crowned** and **Black-and-white Casqued hornbills** stop to call and look around, and you might catch a flash of the bright blue wings of a **Woodland Kingfisher**.

At riverside camp sites and lodges on the Mara River, both inside and outside the reserve, you may be fortunate enough to see the gorgeous turacos (**Schalow's** or the more common **Ross's**), the large **Pel's Fishing Owl** or the **Brown-throated Wattle-eye**. **Northern Black Flycatcher** and barbets, including **Red-fronted**, **Spot-flanked**, **Double-toothed** and **D'Arnaud's** (the race *usambiro*, formerly considered to be a separate species, the Usambiro Barbet), are common throughout the Mara.

With good rains the black cotton soil in the west easily becomes waterlogged, forming grassy seasonal pools that are good for **African Open-billed** (abundant) and **Saddle-billed storks**, **Glossy Ibis**, **Water Thick-knee**, **Greater Painted-snipe**, weavers and bishops. When dry, sedge-fringed ponds form in seasonal rivers attracting the Malagasy migrant **Madagascar Pond Heron** (May–September), **Goliath** (largest heron in the world) and **Purple herons**, **African Water Rail** and **Common Moorhen**. The uncommon **Rufous-bellied Heron** breeds at the Musiara Swamp. Other birds seen near wetlands in the Mara are **Spur-winged Goose**, **Knob-billed Duck**, **Black Coucal** (uncommon), **Lesser Swamp** and **African Reed warblers** and, in season, many migrant waders.

Rufous-bellied Heron crowded in a bush at the Musiara Swamp, Masai Mara

■ *Oloololo Escarpment and the Saparingo Valley:* Rock-loving Cisticola, **Familiar Chat** and **Long-billed Pipit** are found about the boulders strewn on the slopes of the Oloololo Escarpment. Search the escarpment for **Grey-crested Helmetshrike** (presumed to breed in the area), **Lühder's Bushshrike, Grey-winged Robin, Red-capped Robin Chat, White-headed Wood-hoopoe** and local 'specials' – the **Trilling Cisticola** (uncommon), **Pale Wren Warbler** and (seasonally) **Purple-banded Sunbird**.

Birds of prey seen taking advantage of thermal uplifts off the escarpment include **Lanner** and **Peregrine falcons, Bateleur, Ovambo Sparrowhawk** (rare), **Lesser Spotted Eagle** and **Crowned Eagle**. The **White-necked Raven** is also seen above the escarpment.

Birds akin to those of western forests like Kakamega (Site 30) or Nyakweri forests (about 20km beyond the escarpment by way of the C13), such as **Ross's Turaco, Grey-throated Barbet, White-chinned Prinia, Joyful Greenbul, Yellow-throated Leaflove, Yellow-bellied Hyliota** and **Green-capped Eremomela**, do find their way to the woodlands on the Oloololo Escarpment and down into the Saparingo Valley.

OTHER WILDLIFE

Mara has an abundance of herbivores, predators, reptiles, amphibians and insects. A great many animals undertake an epic migration in search of grass around July and August each year, including wildebeest, zebra and gazelles. This journey sees dramatic and heartbreaking crossings at the Mara River. The animals return to the plains of the Serengeti in October or later.

Zebra crossing the Mara River

DUNGA SWAMP IBA

KEY SPECIES
African Skimmer, Blue-spotted Wood Dove, Papyrus Gonolek (E), Carruthers's Cisticola (E), Red-headed Quelea, White-winged Swamp Warbler (E), Papyrus Yellow Warbler (E), Swamp Flycatcher, Red-chested Sunbird, Yellow-backed weaver, Papyrus Canary (E). **Passage migrants:** Gull-billed Tern, White-winged Black Tern.

Dunga Swamp is situated just 10km south of the city of Kisumu at Winam Gulf, Lake Victoria. It extends south of the Dunga Beach fish-landing site for about 5km. Despite the bustling activity on this side of the gulf, papyrus endemics are still found here. (See Yala Swamp, Site 34, for more about papyrus endemics.)

HABITAT
This increasingly fragmented swamp is vegetated largely with papyrus *Cyperus papyrus*, although floating invasives like water hyacinth *Eichhornia crassipes* and water cabbage also occur to various extents at the lake edge.

GETTING THERE
From Kisumu go south on the Jomo Kenyatta Highway to the roundabout that continues straight onto Achieng' Oneko Road. Follow this road for 2.2km, through two roundabouts to a junction that leads onto Ojijo Oteko Road. Turn right into this road and continue for 600m and onto Harambee Road; the tar ends at the junction to the Kenya Wildlife Service Impala Sanctuary. Continue south for 1.1km, passing the Kisumu Yacht Club and the turning to Hippo Point. Bearing right, drive for 1.8km, passing a good many houses before turning right towards the gate for the Dunga Beach Management Unit (BMU).

VISITOR INFO
On entry you soon come to the Dunga Wetland Pedagogical Centre. Here there is a gift shop where you can get information about the conservation of the wetland and enquire about the availability of guides. The boat-landing pier is 100m further along. If you're visiting in the drier months, July–September, when the lake level is lower, you'll be able to hire and go out in one of the rowing boats. Bird guides are available from the local birding group, Lake Victoria Sunset Birders (www.lakevictoriasunsetbirderskenya.org). Contact them on admin@lakevictoriasunsetbirderskenya.org. You may need waterproofs if attempting to wade into the papyrus on foot.

Swamp Flycatcher

Jacques Pitteloud

THE BIRDING

The open fish-landing area attracts large water birds hoping for scraps, including **Reed Cormorant**, **Yellow-billed Stork** and **African Open-billed Stork**. On the peripheral marshes **Grey Crowned Crane** and, in season (September–April), **Gull-billed** and **White-winged Black terns** are common. Occasionally, flocks of **Red-headed Quelea** descend onto the papyrus. Areas of thick papyrus north and south of the landing are hard to access, and it is best to take a guide.

Peter Usher
Black Crake

Away from the busy beach area and about 170m to the right of the landing is a small garden at the lake's edge with open pools adjoining tall papyrus. This is where the local birding group is based. As you weave your way around the houses (which is possible for about a kilometre), check the trees and hedges for **Meyer's Parrot**, **Bare-faced Go-away-Bird**, **Black-billed Barbet**, **Green-headed**, **Olive-bellied** and **Red-chested sunbirds** and the uncommon **Purple Starling** (May–October).

Common lakeside birds seen at the local bird group compound include **Little Bittern**, **Great White**, **Yellow-billed** and **Little egrets**, **Woodland Kingfishers**, **Blue-spotted Wood Dove**, **Eastern Grey Plantain-eater**, **Black-headed Gonolek**, **Village Weaver** and **Yellow-backed Weaver**.

There is a rest banda set close to the payprus where you can sit and watch for **Black Crake**, **Lesser Moorhen**, **Carruthers's Cisticola** and **Swamp Flycatcher**. **Lesser Flamingo** flying high overhead are an unexpected sight, their likely destination being the alkaline Lake Simbi Nyaima, south of the gulf.

Taking a boat out gives you a different view of the papyrus and the chance to seek out **Papyrus Gonolek** (listen for their distinct duet), **Papyrus Yellow Warbler** (very rare) and **Papyrus Canary**. While on the water keep your eyes open for **African Skimmer** and **Pink-backed Pelican**.

Kisumu Impala Sanctuary (managed by Kenya Wildlife Service) and Hippo Point are other points along the same road running down from Kisumu that give access to papyrus areas with similar birds.

OTHER WILDLIFE

Beware of Winam Gulf's many hippos and of the large monitor lizards that commonly occur here.

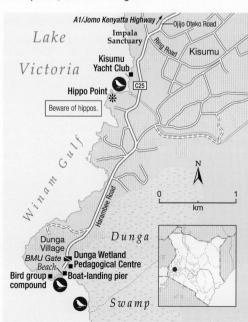

YALA SWAMP IBA

KEY SPECIES

Papyrus Gonolek (E), Carruthers's Cisticola (E), Red-headed Quelea, White-winged Swamp Warbler (E), Papyrus Yellow Warbler (E), Red-chested Sunbird, Copper Sunbird, Papyrus Canary (E).

A number of birds are found in papyrus swamps, but five species occur exclusively in this type of habitat: the **Papyrus Gonolek**, **Carruthers's Cisticola**, **White-winged Swamp Warble**r, **Papyrus Yellow Warbler** and **Papyrus Canary**. In Kenya there are only a few sites with the dense papyrus habitat that these endemic birds require. The largest of these, Yala Swamp, extends across the Yala River Delta in the northeast of Lake Victoria. Lake Kanyaboli is about 10km² and is an oxbow lake that forms an important part of this swamp.

HABITAT

Common reeds and bulrushes grow in the shallower parts of the swamp, while in the deeper regions papyrus *Cyperus papyrus* predominates. The land around the swamp is under intense cultivation, but scattered trees and shrubs occur on the nearby farms. Outlying patches of the swamp are burnt to clear the way for an increasing number of small-scale farms. There are also large areas under irrigation in the northwest and southeast. A dyke tapers off the southern end of Lake Kanyaboli and controls water

A gap in the papyrus provides a view of Lake Kanyaboli.

flow from the lake into the swamp. Other small lakes that lie within the swamp are Lake Sare, a 5km² lagoon in the southwest, and Lake Nyamboyo, situated between lakes Sare and Kanyaboli and measuring only 2km².

GETTING THERE

Yala Swamp can be reached from Siaya town, which is 72km northwest of Kisumu. Drive west out of Siaya on the all-weather Siaya–Kadenge Road (also called the Siaya–Dominion or Siaya–Yimbo road). Keep going, ignoring the Nyandiwa–Yimbo road, and pass the villages of Usenge, Obambo and Nyalula until you get to the Dominion Farm fence. Turn right here. The road skirts the fence and leads you to the causeway.

VISITOR INFO

National reserve status has been proposed for Lake Kanyaboli, but the decision is pending. Papyrus endemics can be found throughout the year, but access may be difficult after heavy rains or flooding. You should be prepared for afternoon rain showers in the area, especially during the rainy seasons.

Currently it is best to overnight in Siaya town, where various types of accommodation are available. You will need to get a very early start, as being out when the roads are quieter and the birds more active greatly improves your chances of seeing endemic species.

For a local guide, contact the Yala Community Ecotourism Organization at yalaecotourism@gmail.com.

THE BIRDING

Begin by heading north at the 2km section of causeway that starts at the Yala River and has tall papyrus on one side and farm fields on the other.

Perched among the papyrus you are likely to see the quick movements of the **Papyrus Gonolek**. Listen for the hollow 'chew, chew, chew' call of the male, which the female answers after a very brief pause. Meanwhile there are usually **weavers**

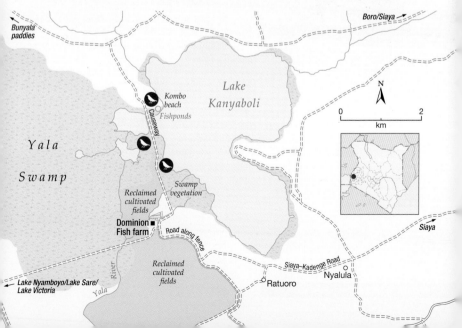

Black-headed Gonolek

African Reed Warbler

(Ploceidae) around, including **Slender-billed, Northern, Brown-throated** (uncommon) and **Compact weavers**, as well as the **Yellow-backed Weaver**, not to be confused with the **Golden-backed**, which is also resident. Other birds to look for along the papyrus edge include **Purple Heron, Black Crake, Blue-headed Coucal, Pied** and **Malachite kingfishers**, Swamp Flycatcher and Red-chested Sunbird. In breeding plumage the uncommon **Southern Red Bishop** is a stunning streak of colour.

Papyrus Canary and **Carruthers's Cisticola**, with its bright brown head, pale-tipped black tail and brown wings, are also likely to be noticed as they call and move among the papyrus.

The openings created when papyrus is harvested can be good places to look for warblers, including **White-winged Swamp Warbler**, the local **Greater Swamp Warbler** and the **African Reed Warbler**. You should also look for **Papyrus Yellow Warbler**, although it is rare nowadays.

In the reclaimed cultivated fields like those on the other side of the causeway, look for **Grey-backed Fiscal**, swallows including **Rufous-chested Swallow**, flocks of **Red-headed Quelea**, **Fan-tailed** and **Yellow-mantled widowbirds** and **Yellow-fronted Canary**. Common sights include **Grey Kestrel**, which takes advantage of the many Hamerkop nests for breeding, **African Black-shouldered Kite** hovering and **Western Banded Snake Eagle**.

Kombo Beach is a fish-landing site that brings you close to the water's edge. It is located a little distance beyond some fishponds to the right of the end of the causeway. In season (October–April) look for **Osprey** and **Gull-billed** and **White-winged Black terns** over the open water.

Birds frequenting the trees and hedges on the margins of farmland away from the swamp include **Red-headed Lovebird, Meyer's Parrot**, woodpeckers, **Black-billed** and **Double-toothed barbets, Marsh Tchagra, Black-headed Gonolek, Yellow-throated Leaflove, Wattled Starling, Scarlet-chested, Olive-bellied** and **Copper sunbirds, Black Bishop** and **Black-rumped Waxbill**.

OTHER WILDLIFE

Lake Kanyaboli is an essential refuge for indigenous tilapia and endangered cichlid fish species, which were once common in Lake Victoria. The papyrus also provides cover for the endangered sitatunga antelope, spotted-necked otter, and – the bane of many farmers' lives – wild pig.

BUNYALA PADDIES

KEY SPECIES

African Open-billed Stork, Grey Kestrel, Beaudouin's Snake Eagle, Western Banded Snake Eagle, Collared Pratincole, Whiskered Tern, Yellow-backed Weaver. **Passage migrants:** Black-tailed Godwit, Common Snipe, White-winged Black Tern.

More than 680ha of paddies make up the rice irrigation scheme of Bunyala, in western Kenya. Every year, a breathtaking spectacle unfolds when the paddies are flooded, and thousands of storks and water birds, **Black-tailed Godwit**, **White-winged Black Tern** and other migrant waders descend to feed.

HABITAT

The Bunyala paddies are situated north of Yala Swamp and south of the Nzoia River, which supplies water for the scheme. Like Mwea (Site 17), this is a large wetland area fed by a system of canals. Grassy paths run between the paddies. Larger canals form freshwater ponds with lilies and morning glories, *Ipomoea*. Many farms bordering the scheme have trees and hedges. As the area is flat with very little vegetation, you get a good view over the paddies, each of which measures about 100m across. (There is also another, larger area of paddies beyond the central block of the scheme.)

GETTING THERE

From Siaya town take the Siaya–Rwambwa–Nyadorera Road (C30) in a westerly direction for 24km, until you reach a Y-shaped junction with a small market centre called 'Junction'. Take the left fork into Rwambwa–Buyuku Road. Rice paddies will come into view on your left and after about 2–3km you will be right in the middle of the central block of the plantation. You can't drive in, so park as best you can along the side of the road.

VISITOR INFO

As with Yala Swamp (Site 34), you should overnight in Siaya town and benefit from an early start. The birding is best during the migration season (September–April) and when the paddies are flooded for planting.

Flooded rice paddies at Bunyala; Beaudouin's Snake Eagle is regularly seen here.

Little Stint and Wood Sandpiper   Black-tailed Godwit

THE BIRDING

Because the Bunyala Rice Scheme is laid out on a uniform grid pattern, you can walk straight for stretches of up to a kilometre with paddies on either side of you. When the paddies are flooded, flocks of whistling ducks, **Knob-billed Duck** and **Glossy Ibis** are common. **Greater Painted-snipe** and, in season, thousands of **Common Snipe** are easy to spot in freshly planted paddies – scan the flooded grassy fields for their bold markings and long bills. **Collared** and rare **Madagascar pratincoles** may also be roosting on the grassy margins of the paddies.

From May to September **African Open-billed Stork**, the Afrotropic migrant **Abdim's Stork** and **Little Egret** are abundant in nearby fields.

In season (September–April) the Bunyala paddies teem with thousands of **White-winged Black Tern**, which typically occur in mixed parties with **Whiskered Tern** and spread out into the planted paddies. The **Gull-billed Tern** occurs in much smaller numbers. Look in the water or on muddy banks for **Black-tailed Godwit**, **Marsh**, **Green**, **Wood** and **Curlew sandpipers**, **Little Stint** and **Ruff**. **Black-winged Stilt** and **Common Greenshank** also occur in large numbers.

The many birds in the paddies tend to attract raptors. Look out for **Peregrine Falcon**, **Western Banded Snake Eagle**, **Gabar Goshawk** and **Ayres's Hawk Eagle**. The Bunyala paddies are also considered the best place in the country to see **Beaudouin's Snake Eagle**.

Come the harvest, and much to the consternation of the farmers in the area, swarms of **Village** and **Yellow-backed weavers**, **Cardinal Quelea** and **Red-billed Quelea** descend.

OTHER WILDLIFE

African serval and African civet are rare nocturnal mammals that occur in the area around the paddies. Rock python and bush snakes also occur.

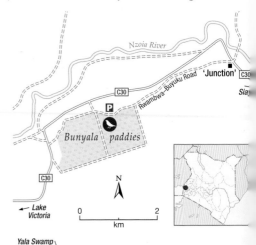

MOUNT ELGON

KEY SPECIES

Black-and-white Casqued Hornbill, Yellow-billed Barbet, Black-throated Wattle-eye, Purple-throated Cuckooshrike, Hunter's Cisticola, Black-collared Apalis, Sharpe's Starling, Green-headed Sunbird, Malachite Sunbird. **Passage migrant:** Tree Pipit.

Mount Elgon, Kenya's second-largest mountain, is an old volcano, the north and west slopes of which actually lie in Uganda. On its Kenyan side most of it is part of a forest reserve. The mountain's base measures approximately 100km in circumference, and its summit, a basalt column called Koitobos, rises to 4,222m. Mount Elgon National Park is off the beaten track, incredibly scenic and is covered with montane forest that is home to 51 highland bird species.

HABITAT

The forests of Mount Elgon National Park include amazing stands of *Podocarpus* and Elgon olive *Olea capensis*. Higher up, dense mountain bamboo is found amid highland forest. Beyond this are heathlands, which may be spectacularly carpeted with the yellow flowers of *Helichrysum* and with scattered giant heather. Higher still, on a trek up to the peaks, there is moorland (at 3,458m), with huge lobelias and giant groundsels *Senecio elgonensis*, which grow up to 7m and are unique to East Africa. Numerous streams run off Mount Elgon and feed the Nzoia and Turwel rivers, which, in turn, empty into Lake Victoria and Lake Turkana respectively.

GETTING THERE

The easiest access is from Kitale: take the Kitale–Suam Road towards Endebess for about 11km. Turn left at the Kenya Wildlife Service sign, and drive for 15km along the corrugated road, past Mount Elgon Lodge and up to the Chorlim Gate.

Alternatively, instead of turning left after 11km, you can continue for a further 6km along the Kitale–Suam Road before turning left through the town of Endebess and driving for 4km on the C44, a murram road, which joins the earlier-mentioned corrugated road. Turn right and drive for another 7km past Mount Elgon Lodge up to the Chorlim Gate. The former route is more scenic and 'birdy', but the road is less comfortable.

VISITOR INFO

An entry fee is payable; remember to take identification. You can book a camp site, banda or guest house in the park, all of which are self-catering. Other overnight options are available in Kitale, including the Kitale Golf Club. Though further away, you could also consider the accommodation options given for Site 37. A four-wheel drive is not necessary, but where the track ends on the moorland, conditions can get boggy.

The beautiful moorlands of Mount Elgon

Yellow-billed Barbet

Malachite Sunbird

THE BIRDING

You can drive along the tracks on Mount Elgon's lower slopes, close to the forest line at about 2,200m, stopping to bird-watch, but be cautious of buffalo and elephant.

Starting at the park office and guest house near Chorlim Gate, take some time in the long open area here to watch for **Cinnamon-chested Bee-eater** and **Black-and-white Casqued** and **Crowned hornbills**, which stop on tall trees. **African Harrier Hawk, Augur Buzzard** and **Crowned Eagle** soar by or circle in search of prey. **Mountain Buzzard**, commonly seen from the forest tracks, may also pass by.

The park has a few camp sites near the Chorlim Gate, which also create a forest edge and open spaces. They are good places to search for **Yellow-billed Barbet, Fine-banded** and **Cardinal woodpeckers, Grey** and **Purple-throated cuckooshrikes, Montane Oriole**, apalis (**Chestnut-throated, Grey** and the tail-wagging **Black-collared**), **Waller's, Stuhlmann's** and **Sharpe's** (uncommon) **starlings, Dusky** and **White-eyed Slaty flycatchers, Black-billed** and **Brown-capped weavers** and in season, October–April, **Willow Warbler, Blackcap** and **Tree Pipit**.

Away from the gate and camps, explore the circuits in the lower part of the park for other highlands birds. Take the track towards the Kassawai Gate (closed), which is south of Chorlim Gate, or head towards the Endebess Bluff and in a northerly direction towards the drier area of the park known as the Elephant Platform. Look out for **White-headed Wood-hoopoe, Black-throated Wattle-eye, Doherty's** and **Lühder's bushshrikes, Cinnamon Bracken** and **Brown Woodland warblers**, greenbuls (**Mountain, Yellow-whiskered, Slender-billed** and **Joyful**), **Mountain Illadopsis**,

Brown-chested Alethe, White-starred and Grey-winged robins and Green-headed, Olive and Northern Double-collared sunbirds.

As you progress up the mountain tracks you may also see little flocks of **Black-crowned** and **Kandt's waxbills** in the grass and bushes, while above you there may be **Mottled Swift** and **Black Saw-wing**. Also look for **Chubb's Cisticola** on the forest edge and near streams.

In the higher forest, which is dominated by giant *Podocarpus*, listen for **Red-fronted Parrot**. There may also be **Abyssinian Ground Thrush**, **Tacazze Sunbird** and **Abyssinian Crimsonwing**. At about this altitude (above 2,500m) you may start to hear **Hunter's Cisticola**.

A track ascends to beautiful open heathlands with grasses, wild flowers and scattered trees. Be on the lookout for **Moorland Francolin**, **Harlequin Quail**, pairs of **White-necked Raven**, **Malachite Sunbird** and **Moorland Chat**. The endangered endemic **Sharpe's Longclaw** has also been recorded on the moorlands.

OTHER WILDLIFE

Blue monkey, black-and-white colobus monkey, zebra, waterbuck, bushbuck and even giant forest hog are regularly seen on the lawns of the guest house and bandas. The 160m-deep Kitum Cave is the site of a rather unusual phenomenon: elephant walk into its dark interior to excavate for salt. If you are interested in viewing this, inform the park warden and request a guide.

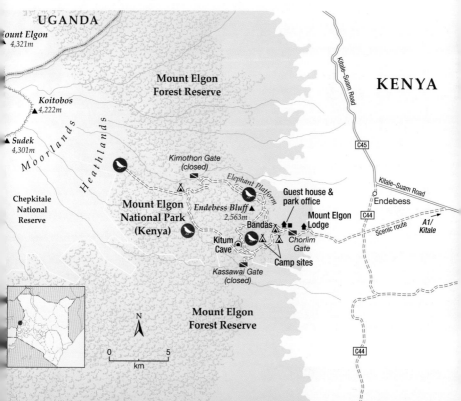

SITE 37

SAIWA SWAMP NATIONAL PARK [IBA]

KEY SPECIES
Buff-Spotted Flufftail, Ross's Turaco, Eastern Grey Plantain-eater, Double-toothed Barbet, Mountain Illadopsis, Splendid Starling, Grey-winged Robin, Red-headed Bluebill.

Saiwa Swamp is a tiny green oasis in northwestern Kenya, surrounded by intensely cultivated smallholder farms. Although it was set up primarily to protect the sitatunga, an endangered semi-aquatic antelope, this park also preserves a habitat that is increasingly threatened and is excellent for the birds of the western Kenyan highlands. This is the only national park where the trails are accessible exclusively by foot.

HABITAT
Saiwa Swamp fringes the Sinyerere River. Only occasional stretches of open water are visible, owing to the lush growth of reeds, sedges and bulrushes. The park is approximately 6km long and no more than about 300m wide. Trails weave through the riparian woodland and small areas of scrub and grass.

Red-headed Bluebill

GETTING THERE
Saiwa Swamp is located north of Kitale, off the road to Kapenguria. From Kitale take the A1 for 18km to the Kipsaina Junction and look out for a Kenya Wildlife Service sign indicating the turn-off for Saiwa Swamp National Park. Turn right off the main road and onto an all-weather murrum road. Drive for about 4.5km to reach another sign, indicating the left turn for the park gate, which is about 500m beyond the sign. If you wish to stay overnight at the park, you will need to pay a vehicle entry fee. Otherwise, park outside the gates.

VISITOR INFO
The park is open daily and national park fees, rules and open times apply. An information centre is located near the entrance to the park. The self-catering Tree Top Hut has views over the swamp and sleeps two, while the Sitatunga public camp site has a lawn, toilets, shower facilities and cooking areas. Alternatively, you may prefer to go 6km further up the main road and stay at Barnleys Guest House or the Sirikwa Safaris camp site in the same grounds (sirikwasafaris.com). The extensive gardens here are also excellent for birds. If you would like a bird guide, ask for Maurice at Sirikwa Safaris. Another option is Crane's 5.3ha Sirwo Farm, located off the C48 from Kitale, near Sibanga town. Their current birding checklist comprises 134 species, including many western and northern specials.

THE BIRDING

It is very pleasant to walk the wooded trails that run along both sides of the river. Explore for **Blue-spotted Wood Dove**, **Great Spotted Cuckoo**, **Narina Trogon**, **Woodland Kingfisher**, **Double-toothed Barbet**, **Brown-backed Woodpecker**, **Black-throated Wattle-eye**, **Grey-headed** and **Lühder's bushshrikes**, **African Blue Flycatcher** and **Green-throated Sunbird**. More

Jacques Pitteloud

Grey-winged Robin

skulking denizens of the dense understorey include **Mountain Illadopsis** and **Grey-winged Robin**. In the early morning listen out for the mournful, single-noted call of the **Buff-Spotted Flufftail**.

A timber walkway takes you across the river and the swamp. **African Water Rail**, **Black Crake**, **Marsh** and **Black-crowned tchagras**, **Little Rush Warblers**, **African Reed Warblers**, **Spectacled**, **Black-billed**, **Holub's Golden** and **Brown-capped weavers** and **Red-headed Bluebill** are likely in the bulrushes and trees around you.

Walking south you will find a well-placed viewing platform that affords an opportunity to look down into the open water. **Yellow-billed Stork**, **Grey** and **Purple heron** and **Grey-crowned Crane** are commonly seen, and this is also the best place to spot a sitatunga.

From the tower, scan the trees on the opposite bank for **Eastern Grey Plantain-eater**, the scarlet flash of **Ross's Turaco**, the **Black-and-white Casqued Hornbill** or the **Splendid** and **Waller's starlings**.

This trail does not loop around, so eventually you will have to backtrack to the timber walkway or join another trail at the swamp crossing and go for a longer bird walk.

OTHER WILDLIFE

This is one of the few places where you have a good chance of spotting De Brazza's monkey and Cape clawless and spotted-necked otters.

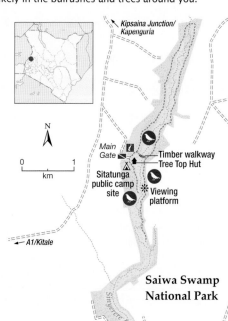

Saiwa Swamp
National Park

KONGELAI ESCARPMENT

KEY SPECIES

White-crested Turaco, Eastern Grey Plantain-eater, Jackson's Hornbill, Yellow-billed Shrike, Lesser Blue-eared Starling, Splendid Starling, Bronze-tailed Starling, Chestnut-crowned Sparrow Weaver, Heuglin's Masked Weaver.

The Kongelai Escarpment is a little-visited area in northwestern Kenya, with over 300 bird species. Many, like the **White-crested Turaco**, **Yellow-billed Shrike** and **Chestnut-crowned Sparrow Weaver**, are specials and are characteristic of the Sudanese and Guinean savanna.

HABITAT

The scenic highlands of the Kongelai Escarpment descend steeply into a remote, semi-arid countryside of acacia and *Combretum* bush. Here pastoralists graze their cattle, and crops are increasingly being cultivated, especially along the banks of the Suam River. The rainfall and birds are strongly linked to the altitude, which ranges from 2,060m down to 1,280m.

GETTING THERE

Travel north of Kitale on the A1 past the turn-off to Saiwa Swamp National Park (Site 37) and continue to the town of Makutano. At Makutano, turn left at the turn-off to Kacheliba and travel across the escarpment and down a 25km descent to the Suam River. The steep, sandy dirt road on the first half of the journey is well worn, mostly by the weight of lorries.

VISITOR INFO

Take plenty of drinking water with you, as temperatures can get to 35°C. (For places to stay, see Sites 36 and 37.) Owing to the many cultivated fields near the Suam River you may find it hard to get access. Explore the track to the right of the main road before the river crossing.

Patrick L'Hoir

Yellow-billed Shrike

The road along the escarpment offers excellent views of the semi-arid bushland beyond.

THE BIRDING

Going slowly along the road out of Makutano will give you the opportunity to note birds that stop on the few fig trees here. These may include **Yellow White-eye, Cinnamon-chested Bee-eater, Fan-tailed Raven** and

Jackson's Hornbill is seen in the dry bushland of northwestern Kenya.

Lesser Blue-eared Starling. Watch out for vehicles and motorcycles if you stop, though.

Turn right at Mtembur, which is about 12.5km from the Makutano turn-off. Remnant woodlands and hedges anywhere here, including along the dry riverbed or *lugga* that is less than 1km down this track, may hold a good selection of the birds of the escarpment. Fairly widespread species include **Crested Francolin, Eastern Grey Plantain-eater, Green Wood-hoopoe, African Grey, Red-billed** and **Jackson's hornbills, Black-headed Gonolek, Northern White-crowned Shrike, Grey-backed Fiscal** and, near to cattle bomas, **Red-billed Oxpecker**. Also listen out for **Brown-backed Woodpecker**.

Kongelai is Kenya's most reliable locality for **Yellow-billed Shrike**. Walking along the dry riverbeds can be a good way to check figs and acacias for **White-crested Turaco** and **Wahlberg's Honeybird**. Look out also for **Lilac-breasted Roller, Spot-flanked** and **D'Arnaud's barbets, Pygmy Batis, Northern Puffback, Black Cuckooshrike, Lead-coloured Flycatcher, Bronze-tailed, Splendid** and **Slender-billed starlings, African Thrush, Marico** and **Shining sunbirds, Chestnut-crowned Sparrow Weaver** and **Heuglin's Masked** (uncommon) and **Red-headed weavers**.

You can continue for another 18km exploring the dry acacia scrub below the escarpment before reaching the Suam River. Look out for **Stone Partridge** on rocky hillsides.

OTHER WILDLIFE

Not much is known of the other wildlife in the area.

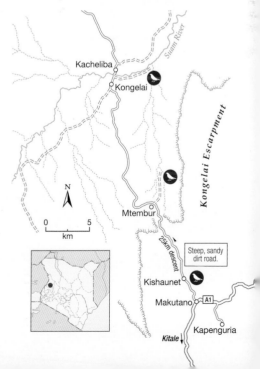

SITE 39

SABAKI RIVER ESTUARY IBA

KEY SPECIES
Broad-billed Sandpiper, Madagascar Pratincole, Sooty Gull, Lesser Crested Tern, Saunders's Tern, African Skimmer.

The mouth of the Sabaki River offers a rich diversity of species (including many rarities) and spectacular numbers of gulls and terns – there are records of up to 500,000 terns roosting here on a single night. They feed far out at sea and return to Sabaki to roost on the sand banks.

HABITAT
Sabaki is the name of the last segment of one of the longest rivers in Kenya, the Athi-Galana-Sabaki. It drains into the Indian Ocean. Approaching the estuary from the road you'll see homesteads and farms, beyond which are sand dunes. Combretums and invasive mesquite *Prosopis juliflora* (known locally as *mathenge*) dot the 130m area of land between the dunes and the beach. Seasonal and permanent wetlands are found on both sides of the dunes, and mangroves grow along parts of the river. Low tide reveals sand banks, deep sticky mud and many fiddler crabs.

GETTING THERE
From Malindi travel north for 5km on the Malindi–Mambrui Road (B8), cross the bridge over the Sabaki, slow down and continue for 200m, passing some village shops. Turn right and a track will take you past the fencing of a parcel of land slated for a golf-course development, around some homesteads and through an opening in the same fence to rejoin an older track from the village. You'll then descend along a sandy path to reach the mud flats by the river. There are no signs. You can start birding 2.6km from the B8 turnoff. It is another 1.7km by foot to the mouth of the river.

VISITOR INFO
The birds are most diverse and numerous during the migration season, September–April. Neap tides bring larger numbers of terns than usual to roost on the exposed sand bars and sand

Storks, ibises, herons and pelicans come to feed on the banks of the Sabaki Rver.

flats on both sides of the river mouth. (It is helpful to have a telescope.) The site is unprotected, and currently there is no charge to enter. This may change if the envisioned conservation efforts succeed. You will want to get an early start, as it can get very hot very quickly as the day progresses. For a local bird guide, enquire at the Nature Kenya office in Gede (nkcoast@naturekenya.org). Unfortunately, sand mining has recently started in the area.

THE BIRDING

Approach the river mouth by walking east, skirting both the mud flats that border the river and an 800m stretch of mangroves. There are sand dunes at the lower end of the mangroves – look out for the tell-tale short cut over the dunes, and you'll come out onto the sand flats about 1km back from the mouth. Note that, depending on whether the river is

Peter Usher

White-fronted Plover (left) and Curlew Sandpiper (right)

in flood or not, the mouth may change quite dramatically in its course and extent.

Against a backdrop of breaking waves that, not infrequently, have hippos surfing in them, you'll quickly spot **Lesser Flamingo**, which gather in larger numbers when the river is low and the estuary less flooded. Although they don't breed here, they are present for most of the year and feed on the mud flats along with a variety of shore birds: **Pied Avocet** (an Afrotropic migrant), **Three-banded** and **White-fronted plovers** and **Collared Pratincole** (which have been known to nest below the dunes).

Sabaki is the best place in the country to see **Madagascar Pratincole**, a threatened Afrotropic Malagasy migrant that is infrequently noted (March–September), and the wintering Palaearctic wader **Broad-billed Sandpiper**, which is found in sloppy, not dry or flooded, mud, far out in the river mouth. Slowly hunt for their short legs and bold markings among the numerous **Curlew Sandpiper**.

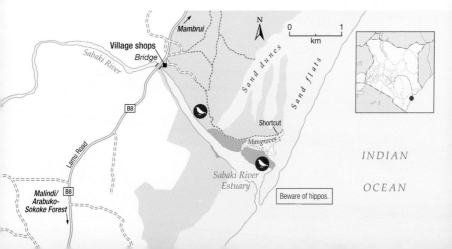

African Skimmer

In season, mixed groups of terns and gulls can include **Sooty Gull** and large numbers of **Lesser Crested** and **Saunders's terns**, as well as **Swift, Roseate** and **White-winged Black terns**. The **White-cheeked Tern** is uncommon in these mixed groups, while the long wings and red beaks of **African Skimmer** make them easy to spot. Not surprisingly, these congregations attract raptors like **Peregrine Falcon, Osprey, African Fish Eagle** and **Western Marsh Harrier** whose appearance causes rapid scattering. Flocks of whistling ducks and **Knob-billed Duck** are among those that you will see regularly taking flight.

Numerous plovers, sandpipers and stints are easiest to see from the mud flats on the riverbanks encountered just before the mangroves. The area just before the mangroves is a good place to see storks, ibises, egrets and **Great White** and **Pink-backed pelicans**. **Black-winged Stilt**, a wet-season species at Sabaki, is found in the freshwater pools that form on the edges of the river.

Look in the scrub as you wind your way along. Terrestrial birds commonly seen away from the

Zanzibar Red Bishop

river include **Blue-cheeked Bee-eater** (a Palaearctic migrant, mainly October–November) and the Afrotropic migrant **White-throated** (May–September) and **Northern Carmine bee-eaters** (November–February). Others include **Black-headed Batis, Black Cuckooshrike** (May–October), **Rufous Chatterer, Spotted Palm Thrush, Purple-banded Sunbird** and the rare **Violet-breasted Sunbird**. Look out also for the notable **Zanzibar Red Bishop** (in breeding plumage, May–October) and **Golden Pipit** (an uncommon visitor from inland). From October to April this scrub is also good habitat for migrant shrikes and wheatears.

OTHER WILDLIFE

Grunting in the early morning is a reminder that hippos are never very far away. Although little is done on this beach to protect them, sea turtles still attempt to nest along the beach, and there may be suni and duiker in the thickets.

DAKATCHA WOODLAND FORESTS IBA

KEY SPECIES
Fischer's Turaco, Chestnut-fronted Helmetshrike, Mouse-coloured Sunbird, Pale Batis, Clarke's Weaver (E), Sokoke Pipit (E).

This extensive area of forest, woodland and farmland is beyond the town of Marafa, northwest of Malindi. Only in the *Brachystegia* woodlands here and at Arabuko-Sokoke Forest to the south is the Kenyan endemic **Clarke's Weaver** found. Dakatcha Woodland Conservation Group spent years searching intensively for the nesting site of this endemic before finally discovering it in 2013. A wide variety of coastal birds can also be seen here.

HABITAT
Dakatcha is a surprisingly varied area of open miombo woodland. It is dominated by *Brachystegia spiciformis* (known locally as *mrihi*) and dotted with gorgeous flowering desert rose *Adenium obesum*. Where *Cynometra webberi (mfunda)* and *Brachylaena huillensis (muhuhu)* trees previously grew – usually on higher ground – thickets and a scattering of active and abandoned

pineapple fields now occur. Along the rivers and valleys there are wetlands and patches of mixed forest, and the gentle hills of the countryside show evidence of dramatic erosion.

GETTING THERE
Travel north of Malindi on the Malindi–Mambrui–Lamu Road, cross the Sabaki River Bridge and take the left turn to Marafa (50km away), the main trading centre in the Dakatcha area. The all-weather murram road passes through Magarini and Marikebuni (where there is a cess barrier, where traders have to pay a levy).

Joining this road at Marikebuni is an almost parallel, less frequented, smoother, and more scenic murram road. To get onto it you'll have to drive 12km from Malindi, then 200m past the Mambrui turn-off, and turn left. (The road has various signposts for Marafa.)

This is the kind of wetland habitat at Dakatcha in which Clarke's Weaver may be found nesting.

VISITOR INFO

The interlinking sandy tracks through Dakatcha's woods and thickets are narrow, with no signposts anywhere, making it difficult to give or get directions, and it is easy to get lost. On some tracks there are also pockets of soft sand, and you will need a four-wheel drive to get through. It is best to hire a guide from the Dakatcha Woodland Conservation Group. Contact them at the Resource Centre at Marafa (dakatchawoodland2015@gmail.com) or via the Nature Kenya offices in Gede (nkcoast@naturekenya.org).

It is pleasant to camp in the woods, although you should contact the Dakatcha Woodland Conservation Group to request permission from the community. However, there is also basic lodging in Marafa, at PJ Lodge, for example. If your time is limited you can stop at the Hell's Kitchen site at Marafa and go birding along the nearby Deka River, where **Fischer's Turaco** and **Trumpeter Hornbill** are commonly observed. Hell's Kitchen is a dramatic depression (known locally as a *nyari*) resulting from extreme soil erosion that has left towering remnants of red magarini soil.

THE BIRDING

Although **Clarke's Weaver** feeds in *Brachystegia* woodland forest, it prefers to nest in wetlands with extensive sedge and grass, a fact that was first discovered in 2013. **Grosbeak Weaver**, found at many wetlands in the area, were nesting in the same habitat, and there was a flock of the seldom-seen **Red-headed Quelea**. During the rainy season therefore, it is worth searching small wetlands that are scattered in the area for signs of nesting.

Wetlands are also good places to look for **Zanzibar Red Bishop** and **Eastern Golden** and **Golden Palm weavers**. Search the scrub close to wetlands and trees around cultivated maize fields for **Northern Brownbul**, **Purple-banded Sunbird** and **Lesser Masked** and **Village weavers**.

Chestnut-fronted Helmetshrike

Jacques Pitteloud

Sokoke Pipit is recorded at a few sites on the East African coast and is globally endangered.

There is extensive *Brachystegia* woodland and you can drive for many kilometres on sandy tracks, stopping to explore on foot when you see movement. Often this movement will turn out to be a mixed party that may include **Common Scimitarbill**, **Mombasa Woodpecker**, **Retz's** and **Chestnut-fronted helmetshrikes** and **Black-bellied** and **Violet-backed** (Afrotropic migrant, March–September) **starlings**. Brachystegias lose their leaves in the dry season, so it is easier to track down sounds or movements at this time. Other birds occurring in the area include **Red-fronted Tinkerbird**, **Pale Batis**, **Pale** and **Spotted** (in season, October–April) **flycatchers**, **Mouse-coloured Sunbird**, **Sokoke Pipit** (endangered), bee-eaters and orioles.

Crested Francolin, **Black-headed Batis**, **Black-crowned Tchagra** and **Zanzibar Greenbul** are commonly heard, as is the shy and uncommon **Eastern Nicator** and the sweet song of the **Bearded Scrub Robin**. **Black-headed Apalis** is typically heard calling from inaccessible *Cynometra* trees. While camping at night, you'll hear the calls the **African Barred Owlet** and **Fiery-necked Nightjar**.

OTHER WILDLIFE

Dakatcha is home to the four-toed and golden-rumped sengis (elephant-shrews), which may quickly zip across your track.

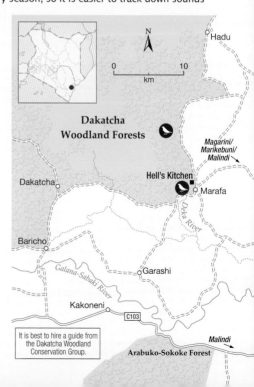

It is best to hire a guide from the Dakatcha Woodland Conservation Group.

ARABUKO-SOKOKE FOREST ▣ IBA

KEY SPECIES

Southern Banded Snake Eagle, Fischer's Turaco, Sokoke Scops Owl, Mombasa Woodpecker, African Broadbill, Little Yellow Flycatcher, Tiny Greenbul, Red-tailed Ant Thrush, Spotted Ground Thrush, East Coast Akalat, Plain-backed Sunbird, Amani Sunbird, Clarke's Weaver (E), Sokoke Pipit.

Arabuko-Sokoke is the largest remnant of coastal forest (420km²) in East Africa and is world renowned for its diversity of animals, plants, amphibians and butterflies, several of which are found only here. It is also one of the most important bird hot spots on the continent, with five globally endangered species – **Sokoke Scops Owl**, **Spotted Ground Thrush**, **Amani Sunbird**, **Clarke's Weaver** and **Sokoke Pipit**.

HABITAT

Situated on the north coast, the forest is made up of bands of distinctly different vegetation. In the northeast and southeast there is mixed forest, with species such as the evergreen gum copal, which has striking white flowers, and remnant *Afzelia quanzensis* (called *mbamba-kofi*), which has far-reaching branches. Woodlands of *Brachystegia spiciformis* (or *mrihi*), spread up and down the middle of the forest,

their dark trunks contrasting with the sandy white soil. They have beautiful open crowns and grow among grasses and flowering shrubs. The remaining 60 per cent of the forest is on sandy red magarini soil and is dominated by *Cynometra* and *Brachylaena* trees.

GETTING THERE

Although contiguous with Mida Creek (Site 42), the forest and trails are on the northern side of the Mombasa–Malindi (B8) highway. Gede Forest Station Gate is the main point of entry. It is located directly off the B8, about 1.6km west of the turn-off to Gede town.

VISITOR INFO

You can hire a guide and pay your entry fee at the visitors' office at Gede Forest Station (open 06h00–18h00). Bear in mind that if you are planning to enter the park early via another point, you will need to pay for your tickets in advance at the Gede Station. To organize a guide ahead of time, contact the Nature Kenya office in Gede (nkcoast@naturekenya.org).

Ask at the station about the condition of the trails, which may be obstructed by fallen branches. Four-wheel drive vehicles are best, but are not strictly necessary unless you are travelling a long distance from your entry point. Note also that during the main rainy season (April–June) horseflies occur in the forest, which you can only hope to avoid. Be mindful, too, of the presence of elephant and of increasing numbers of buffalo and baboon.

Brachystegia spiciformis has a beautiful open crown.

THE BIRDING

You can get some good birding done in the short distance (1.5km) from the KFS ticket office to the forest edge. Walk or drive past the station's village for forestry staff. The eucalyptus plantations and secondary forest here can include **Tambourine Dove**, **African Green Pigeon**, **Fischer's Turaco** (uncommon), **Böhm's Spinetail**, **Mangrove Kingfisher**, **Common Scimitarbill**, **Trumpeter Hornbill**, **Green Barbet**, **Pallid Honeyguide**, **African Golden Oriole**, **Scaly Babbler** and **Black-bellied Starling**.

Green Barbet

Alternatively, take advantage of an early morning start by heading directly to the forest edge, where the trails begin. Going off to the left is the start of the Nature Trail, a 4km circular walk off the main Sand Quarry and Elephant trails. In the middle and low canopy of this mixed forest **African Pygmy Kingfisher** (an Afrotropical migrant, May–November), **African Broadbill**, **Forest Batis**, **Blue-mantled Crested Flycatcher** and **Olive Sunbird** are usually noted along with **Tiny** and **Fischer's greenbuls** and both species of brownbul. In the early morning quiet listen for the foraging sounds that may indicate the presence of **East Coast Akalat**, **Red-capped Robin Chat** (residents occur, although it is an Afrotropical migrant, April–November) or the **Bearded Scrub Robin**. It is rare to see the **Spotted Ground Thrush**, an endangered Afrotropic migrant present only from April–November.

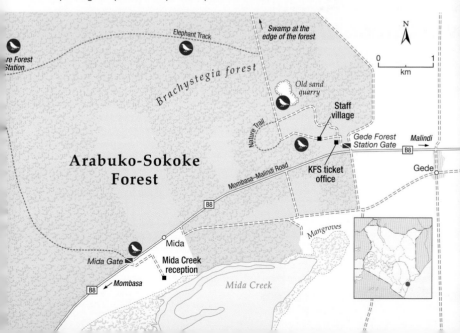

Going right on entry into the forest takes you down the more often birded track leading to the old sand quarry. It also goes through mixed forest, passing the exit to the Nature Trail after about 300m. Look out for **Red-tailed Ant Thrush** and the endangered **Sokoke Pipit**, which are usually seen on the leaf litter on the ground or perched low in the undergrowth. Then comes a stretch frequented by the golden-rumped sengi (elephant-shrew), which dives for cover at the slightest movement.

You'll notice the habitat opening up to your right as you pass through an area where silica sand was once mined. **Southern Banded Snake** and **Crowned eagles**, **African Goshawk** and **Great Sparrowhawk** may be seen here. During the rains seasonal pools form and attract **African Spoonbill**, **Hamerkop**, herons and egrets.

Sokoke Scops Owl

The Elephant Track is about 10km long, circling round and ending at the Mida Gate, back on the Mombasa–Malindi Road (but south of the Gede Forest Station). This is a popular access point for birding in the forest, but ask at the visitors' office beforehand if you plan to enter or exit here, as you may need to collect the gate keys first.

If you are entering at the Mida Gate, go slowly after passing through the elephant barrier: in the very early morning **Peters's Twinspot** is regularly seen on the track, and the trilling call of the **Fiery-necked Nightjar** is heard sporadically.

Drive for about 1.3km, then head northwest for another 2km, towards Jilore Forest Station, to reach the more open *Brachystegia* forest where **Narina Trogon**, **Scaly-throated Honeyguide**, **Little Yellow Flycatcher**, **Yellow-bellied** and **Tiny greenbuls** and **Plain-backed Sunbird** are likely. A mixed feeding party can very quickly liven up the birding. Such parties commonly include **Mombasa Woodpecker**, **Pale Batis**, **Retz's** and **Chestnut-fronted helmetshrikes**, **Gorgeous Bushshrike**, **Amani Sunbird** and **Dark-backed Weaver**. **Clarke's Weaver** is a Kenyan endemic that is frequently found in these mixed parties, most often in the dry months when it is not breeding.

Only in dense *Cynometra* thickets will you find the irresistible **Sokoke Scops Owl**, Africa's smallest owl, but it is worth making an extra effort to locate it. The services of a guide will vastly improve your chances of observing the birds in this forest.

OTHER WILDLIFE

Arabuko-Sokoke Forest is home to the golden-rumped sengi (elephant-shrew) and the very elusive Aders's duiker and Sokoke bushy-tailed mongoose. Almost a third of Kenya's butterflies, over 240 species, have been recorded here.

MIDA CREEK 🔲

KEY SPECIES
Dimorphic Egret, Crab-plover, Lesser Sand Plover, Greater Sand Plover, Terek Sandpiper, Bar-tailed Godwit, Eurasian Curlew (eastern race).

The 6km-long Mida Creek is among the best places in the country to view shore birds and is a popular birding spot, where locals come to see an exciting variety of waders, terns and other water birds, including **Crab-plover**, **Eurasian Curlew** and **Terek Sandpiper**.

HABITAT

The mangroves surrounding most of Mida Creek extend inland for hundreds of hectares. At low tide, extensive sand flats are exposed, providing feeding grounds for thousands of passage and migrant waders. The twice daily tides

and the fresh water received from underground seepage also provide food and habitat for fish, shrimps, crustaceans, molluscs and turtles.

GETTING THERE

Mida Creek is 25km from Malindi. Travel south on the main road to Mombasa (B8), then turn from the main road onto a sandy track to your left, which is marked by a wooden sign with a straw roof that reads 'Mida Creek Mangrove Walkway & Bird Hide, by A Rocha Kenya'. Drive for 150m and turn left – there are one or two places where

When the tide goes out broad expanses of sand are revealed at Mida Creek.

the track links up with other tracks, but continue straight for about 500m until the sandy track curves gently to the right and goes towards the creek. Stop and park beside the small hut that serves as the reception banda for the boardwalk and bird hide.

VISITOR INFO

You can walk out onto the beach and sand flats just a few metres away. If you intend walking out across the sand flats, you should bring diving soles. Note that both soles and telescopes are available for hire at reception.

At reception you can also request a guide or pay to use the 260m suspended boardwalk, which passes through the mangrove forest. There is a bird hide at the end of this boardwalk, which provides excellent cover for viewing. If you don't want to use the suspended boardwalk there are stairs below the bird hide, which you can reach by walking across the sand flats when the tide is out. You can also see the creek by canoe (enquire at reception).

The best time of year to visit is in season, September–March, when waders are present in large numbers.

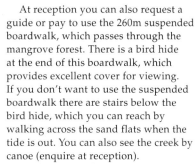

Saunders's Tern

THE BIRDING

The best birding is from the bird hide, starting 30–45 minutes before a neap high tide of 2.3–2.5m. Otherwise, try to arrive just before or after high tide, when the water has receded or is receding and roosting birds are closer for observation. In season up to 10,000 waders can gather close to shore – **Grey Plover, Little Stint, Terek** and **Curlew sandpipers** being the most numerous. **Lesser** and **Greater Sand plovers** may also be abundant, in addition to the common **Gull-billed, Lesser Crested** and **Saunders's terns.** Though a few are present along the coast year-round, almost a thousand **Crab-plovers** roost at Mida Creek in December and January.

Mida Creek is an important roosting site for Crab-plovers.

A mixed flock of Curlew Sandpiper, Greater Sand Plover and Terek Sandpiper

Among the larger parties, try to pick out **Bar-tailed Godwit, Whimbrel, Eurasian Curlew** and **Ruddy Turnstone**.

You are also likely to spot the odd **Yellow-billed Stork, Great White** and **Dimorphic egrets**, wintering **Osprey** working the shoreline, **Common Ringed** and **White-fronted plovers, Sanderlings** (running constantly back and forth as they feed) and hovering **Pied Kingfisher**. There are also small numbers (up to about 300 birds) of **Greater Flamingo, Woolly-necked Stork** and occasional **Black** and **Goliath herons**.

The mangroves further from shore are also interesting. Representative land birds of the north-coast beachfront include **Pale Batis, Chestnut-fronted Helmetshrike, African Golden** and **Black-headed orioles, Black-bellied Starling, Purple-banded Sunbird** and **Golden Palm Weaver**. Numerous **Eurasian Golden Oriole, Willow Warbler** and **Yellow Wagtail** may be present on their northward migration from February to April. The raptors may include **Peregrine Falcon, African Fish Eagle, Wahlberg's Eagle, Ayres's Hawk Eagle, Great Sparrowhawk** and **Lizard Buzzard**.

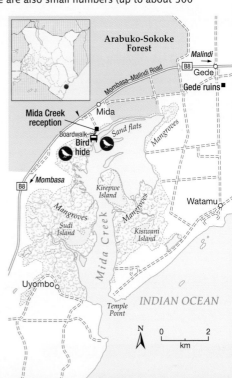

OTHER WILDLIFE

The mangroves are home to a range of reptiles, and the marsh mongoose may also be seen.

HALLER PARK

KEY SPECIES
Black-crowned Night Heron, Goliath Heron, Palm-nut Vulture, African Harrier Hawk, Narina Trogon, Giant Kingfisher, Black-throated Wattle-eye.

Haller Park in Mombasa, on the Kenyan coast, was originally a worked-out lime quarry, but now boasts trees, large lakes and waterways. It is a haven for birds in this otherwise heavily built-up area, where natural habitat is fast disappearing.

HABITAT
Work to transform the quarry wasteland began in 1971. Haller Park now measures 2km², and its plant life is dominated by *Azadirachta indica, Conocarpus lancifolius* and Australian pine tree *Casuarina equisetifolia.*

The striking Giant Kingfisher is the largest kingfisher in Africa.

Water lilies grow in ponds teeming with fish and frogs and fringed with bulrushes and mangrove trees.

GETTING THERE
Haller Park is situated on the Mombasa–Malindi Road, north of the Nyali Bridge. There are two entrances, one on the Mombasa–Malindi Road, the other off the road leading to the Bamburi Cement Factory. The park is well signposted. Both entrances have plenty of safe parking.

VISITOR INFO
The park offers various attractions, including a palm garden, animal and crocodile enclosures and afternoon giraffe, hippo and crocodile feedings. It is here that, in 2005, an orphaned baby hippo called Owen developed an unlikely friendship with a 130-year-old tortoise called Mzee. The park is open to the public from 09h00 to 17h00 daily, and an entry fee is payable. As coastal birds are best seen in the early mornings, you will need to request permission to enter the park earlier than 09h00.

African Fish Eagles are known for their distinctive call.

THE BIRDING

Haller Park is attractive to birds, since the alien **Indian House Crow**, which is prevalent at the coast and a serious predator of eggs and young birds, is less common here.

The park is well laid out, with clearly defined paths. You will find most species of heron and egret, including the magnificent **Goliath Heron** and the **Black-crowned Night Heron**, which roost in the trees along the pathways, especially near the crocodile pool. The **African Harrier Hawk** nests in the tall trees here.

Check the pond in the large animal enclosure, as it is the best place to see the **African Fish Eagle** and **Palm-nut Vulture**. Throughout the park you will see **Grey-headed**, **Mangrove**, **Malachite** and **Pied kingfishers**. Also watch for an infrequent visitor, the **Giant Kingfisher**.

Tall *Casuarina* trees may have **Madagascar** and **Northern Carmine bee-eaters**, Afrotropic migrants that appear from May to September and September to March respectively. In season (November–March) **Eurasian Golden Oriole** and **Eurasian bee-eaters** are commonly seen.

Little Bittern (uncommon) and **Black-throated Wattle-eye** inhabit the reeds and bushes around the ponds, where there may also be a profusion of weavers, sunbirds and seedeaters. The **Narina Trogon** is occasionally seen in the forest near the staff canteen.

OTHER WILDLIFE

See Site 44 (Nguuni Nature Sanctuary) for introduced animals that are also seen at Haller Park. Other wildlife includes civet and genet, monitor lizards and snakes, dragonflies and butterflies. There is a butterfly house in the forest opposite Bamburi Beach Hotel.

Peter Steward

Madagascar Bee-eater

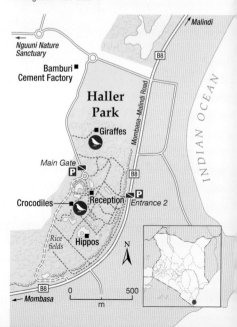

NGUUNI NATURE SANCTUARY

KEY SPECIES
Palm-nut Vulture, Grey-headed Kingfisher, Striped Kingfisher, Malachite Kingfisher, Grey-headed Bushshrike, Sulphur-breasted Bushshrike, African Bare-eyed Thrush, Zanzibar Red Bishop. **Passage migrants:** Many Eurasian migrants.

Owing largely to the presence of the Indian House Crow, there are very few places in or near Mombasa where you can still see a variety of birds, so Nguuni is a welcome surprise for many birders. Its ponds and gently undulating grassland host well over 100 species.

HABITAT
Nguuni was a sheep farm located on Nguu Tatu (Three Hills) that has been developed by the Baobab Trust. It is grassy, with acacia and palm trees, several ponds and a large artificial wetland. There is a shantytown to the south.

GETTING THERE
From Mombasa, get onto the B8 just before the Nyali Bridge, and drive for 8.5km towards Malindi, then turn left onto the road towards the Bamburi Cement Factory and follow it for about 4.5km to the Bamburi Mwisho Junction. Turn right, continue for about 300m, and then turn left. Veer left at the Turkey Base Inn and continue for another 100m. The sanctuary's Main Gate will be to your left before the start of the quarry road. If you are unfamiliar with the road, it may be better to take a taxi.

VISITOR INFO
Early mornings and mid- to late afternoons, after the heat of the day, are the best times to visit. Try to avoid the weekend crowds. There is an entry fee and parking is available. Walking around is the best way to see lots of birds. Giraffe wander freely and are very curious, so if you're on foot, take care not to let them get too close – ask for a guide at reception.

Pangani Longclaw

THE BIRDING

From the entry, follow the trail to your right, which passes a series of ponds and leads to the artificial wetland. Here, waders enjoy the shallows in season (October–April), while **White-faced Whistling Duck**, **Woolly-necked Stork**, **Black Crake** and **Water Thick-knee** are present for most of the year, sometimes in good numbers. **Grosbeak**, **Eastern Golden** and **Golden Palm weavers** breed in colonies around the wetland, along with **Zanzibar Red Bishop**.

A dash of colour at a pond's edge is most likely to be a **Malachite Kingfisher**, diving to nab an insect or small fish before returning to its perch. The ponds also attract **Madagascar Pond Heron** (May–September), which roost in the reeds and palm trees, as well as **Purple Swamphen** and **Allen's Gallinule**.

The adjacent woodlands often have **Grey-headed** and **Sulphur-breasted bushshrikes** and **African Bare-eyed Thrush**. Soaring overhead there may be **Red-necked** and **Peregrine falcons**, **African Black-shouldered Kite**, **Palm-nut Vulture**, **Black-chested Snake Eagle**, **Long-crested Eagle** and, in season, an occasional **Booted Eagle**. Also in season, **Red-backed** and **Isabelline shrikes** may be hunting from perches closer to the ground. The **Eurasian Golden Oriole** is easy to spot as it flies rapidly back and forth between the trees.

Peter Usher

Peregrine Falcon

Trace your steps back to the Main Gate or find your way to the secondary tracks that go past further ponds and woodland in the west. Check the grassy patches close to the tracks for **Yellow-throated** and **Pangani longclaws**, and keep an eye out for **Grey-headed** and **Striped kingfishers** and **Greater Blue-eared** and **Superb starlings** that stop in the trees. The large **Verreaux's Eagle Owl** likes to roost in the doum palms by day. In the evening listen out for the sonar-like call of **Slender-tailed Nightjar**.

OTHER WILDLIFE

In addition to the giraffe, animals that have been introduced to Nguuni include waterbuck, ostrich, eland and oryx. Beautiful leopard orchids (now a protected species) grow on the doum palms.

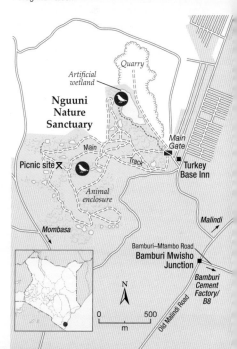

SHIMBA HILLS NATIONAL RESERVE IBA

KEY SPECIES
Crested Guineafowl, Red-necked Spurfowl, Southern Banded Snake Eagle, Fischer's Turaco, Eastern Green Tinkerbird, Green-headed Oriole, Croaking Cisticola, Little Yellow Flycatcher, Fischer's Greenbul, Tiny Greenbul, Plain-backed Sunbird, Uluguru Violet-backed Sunbird.

Rising above the coastal plains south of Mombasa are the Shimba Hills. The Shimba Hills National Reserve is a mosaic of lush lowland coastal forest, grassland, swampy wetland, river valleys and plantations, with well over 100 bird species, including a number of range-restricted birds.

HABITAT
The hills offer excellent views of the surrounding countryside, as well as great diversity and endemism in plants, butterflies and other wildlife. Various forest types grow on the sandy soils produced by the local Shimba Grits and Mazeras sandstone. These include pine plantations, rainforest and drier forest. Along the roads and in the open glades there are glorious wild flowers and the sweetly scented star-like flowers of shrub magnolias *Tabernaemontana*. There are stands of *Raphia farinifera*, a short-stemmed palm with exceptionally long leaves, and of wild date *Phoenix reclinata*. Majestic *Borassus aethiopum* palms tower over woody grassland.

GETTING THERE
Driving south from Mombasa, use the Likoni Ferry to cross from Mombasa Island onto the Likoni–Ukunda Road (A14). Follow this road for 16km until you reach the junction to Kombani town, where there is a signpost for Kwale and Shimba Hills National Reserve. Turn right here onto the Kwale Road (C106) and drive past Kwale town and the electric elephant fence to the Main Gate.

VISITOR INFO
Shimba Hills National Reserve is managed by the Kenya Wildlife Service, and an entry fee is payable. You may be interested in the daily ranger-led walks to the Sheldrick Falls, although they are not particularly 'birdy'. These take place in the warmer part of the day and last for a few hours. Enquire at the gate when you enter.

Inside the reserve there are camping sites as well as bandas that share a well-equipped kitchen. In the forest northwest of the Main Gate there is Shimba Hills Lodge (www.shimbalodge.net), a 'tree hotel' overlooking a waterhole.

Red-necked Spurfowl, Croaking Cisticola and Zanzibar Red Bishop occur in Shimba Hills grassland like this.

THE BIRDING

The track from the Main Gate into the reserve leads through plantations that are alive with swallowtail butterflies. Tall trees host **Black-backed Puffback** and **Green-headed Oriole**. In addition, there are **Zanzibar Sombre** and **Yellow-bellied greenbuls**, although they can be difficult to see, and the coastal **Tropical Boubou**. **Tambourine Dove** and **Emerald-spotted Wood Dove** feed on the road and in the nearby undergrowth, while up above there may be **Böhm's Spinetail**.

Green-headed Oriole

The park requires that you stay in your car, except at designated spots, which makes forest birding tricky, but do your best around the edges of the forest and at picnic sites and viewing points. Look in the trees around the Makadara picnic site for **Green Pigeon**, **Yellowbill**, the beautiful **Fischer's Turaco**, **Green Tinkerbird** and **sunbirds** (**Plain-backed**, the range-restricted **Uluguru Violet-backed**, **Collared** and **Olive**). Lower in the canopy look for **Little Yellow Flycatcher**, **Black-headed Apalis**, **Yellow-bellied**, **Fischer's** and **Tiny greenbuls**, **Red-tailed Ant Thrush** and **Ashy Flycatcher**. You may be fortunate enough to come across the unusual and uncommon **African Broadbill**, which flies in tight little display circles uttering its distinctive call.

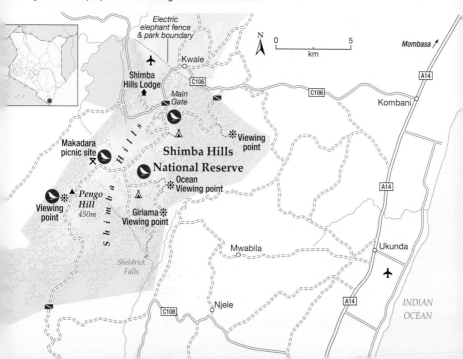

Brown-hooded Kingfisher

Crowned, **Trumpeter** and **Silvery-cheeked hornbills** can often be seen flying below Pengo Hill, the highest point in the reserve (450m), which offers scenic views overlooking forest and palm groves. Listen and look out for **Klaas's Cuckoo**, **Common Scimitarbill**, parties of **Retz's** and **Chestnut-fronted helmetshrikes**, **Black-bellied Starling** and **Dark-backed Weaver**.

A patchwork of grasslands lies between the forests, and here you can watch for **Little Bee-eaters**, the Afrotropic migrant **White-throated** (May–September) and **Northern Carmine** (November–February) **bee-eaters**, skulking **White-browed Coucal**, **Zanzibar Red Bishop** and **Pin-tailed Whydah** (hard to miss in its breeding plumage). Singing from the bushes there may also be **Rattling**, **Croaking** and **Siffling cisticolas**.

Other birds include the scarce **Lesser Cuckoo** (in season, November–April), **Narina Trogon**, **White-eared**, **Green** and **Brown-breasted barbets**, **Grey-headed**, **Brown-hooded**, **Striped** and (near Sheldrick Falls if you are really lucky) **Giant kingfishers**. **Flappet Lark** can be heard flapping and seen diving down towards the grass. Both **Yellow-throated** and **Pangani longclaws** and **Red-necked Spurfowl** also occur. **Common Cuckoo** and **Eurasian Golden Oriole** are known to pass through on their northward migration (March–April) in impressive numbers. Shimba Hills Lodge is a good place to find the shy **Crested Guineafowl**, the **African Fish Eagle** and the **African Wood Owl**. The lodge is often also the best place to see **Green-headed Oriole**.

Resident raptors include **Southern Banded Snake Eagle**, **Bateleur**, **Great Sparrowhawk**, **Grasshopper Buzzard** (an Afrotropic migrant) and **Crowned Eagle**. The **Palm-nut Vulture** is common and delightful to watch when displaying.

OTHER WILDLIFE

It is only in this small reserve that the rare and striking Roosevelt sable antelope *Hippotragus niger roosevelti* is found. The hills are important for two endemic reed frog species, black and rufous sengi and a race of bushy-tailed mongoose. They are also home to troops of Angolan black-and-white colobus, herds of elephant and buffalo, and the red-bellied coast squirrel. Furthermore, the hills and surrounding forest reserves are an amazing hot spot for butterflies and plants.

SITE 46

MOMBASA ROAD

KEY SPECIES
African Darter, White-backed Vulture, Black-faced Sandgrouse, Pearl-spotted Owlet, Abyssinian Scimitarbill, Red-capped Lark, Red-capped Robin Chat, Marico Sunbird, Black-bellied Sunbird, Eastern Golden Weaver, Golden Palm Weaver, African Quailfinch, Eastern Paradise Whydah, Steel-blue Whydah, Golden Pipit.

The 473km-long A109 between Nairobi and Mombasa is one of the busiest stretches of road in the country. It links the port city of Mombasa with the capital and with the wider region and sees a constant stream of cars, buses, trucks and long-haul trailers. It may be a far cry from the ox-cart track it was in 1896, but it is still a long and challenging drive. If that doesn't daunt you, there is some great birding to be had at various spots along this route.

HABITAT
Nowadays Nairobi seems to extend a long way down Mombasa Road before you reach the grasslands of the Athi-Kapiti Plains. Large farms and ranches devoted to conservation, livestock grazing or both alternate with towns and settlements. Birding hot spots along this road include the golden grasslands of the Athi-Kapiti Plains, the green woodlands around Kiboko, the groundwater forest of Kibwezi and the dense Tsavo thorn-bush (*nyika*) dotted with baobabs.

GETTING THERE
The best-known towns along the Mombasa Road – Sultan Hamud, Emali, Makindu and Mtito Andei – were major stations on the Kenya Railway Line, which was completed in 1901. Later, when the road was constructed, they functioned as milestones for weary travellers or motorists in need of help. Detailed directions are given below, along with the birding descriptions at each key stop along this route.

VISITOR INFO
If you are going back to Nairobi, be prepared for the traffic on the return journey. The car journey between Nairobi and Mombasa is about seven hours. You may prefer to start in Mombasa or Malindi if you are visiting sites further down Mombasa Road or at the coast. You can take the train from Nairobi to Mombasa or take the one-hour flight.

Peter Steward

Eastern Paradise and Straw-tailed whydahs and Red-billed Quelea drinking at a waterhole

THE BIRDING

■ *The Athi-Kapiti Plains:* A good place to view the birds of these gently undulating grassland plains is the Swara Plains Ranch, which is 36km from Nairobi on the right-hand side of the road, next to Small World Country Club and before the Lukenya rock face. You can pay a fee to enter for the day or stay overnight at the Swara Plains Acacia Camp (swaraplains.com). If you are at the ranch after the rains, check the muddy edges of seasonal wetlands for **African Quailfinch** and look in the surrounding sedge for the bumbling **Yellow-crowned Bishop**. In the scrub nearby one can find **Water Thick-knee**, and **Grey Crowned Crane** have been known to nest on the islands in the many dams. A walk through the scrub and among the yellow fever trees *Acacia xanthophloea* at the Swara Plains Acacia Camp can turn up a good variety of birds, among them hornbills, barbets, sunbirds, the critically endangered **White-backed Vulture**, which nests here, **Abyssinian Scimitarbill** and **Red-throated Tit**. Thrush and **Common nightingales** may both be seen in season (November–March).

A drive through the grasslands is likely to turn up bustards, larks and more raptors. Look on or beside the tracks for **Spotted Thick-knee, Temminck's Courser, Black-faced Sandgrouse, Rufous-naped, Red-capped, Short-tailed** and **Fischer's sparrow larks,** the common **Grassland Pipit,** and, in season, storks and **Isabelline, Northern** and **Pied wheatears.**

■ *Hunter's Lodge:* This lodge (www.madahotels.com/index.php/hunters-lodge-fact-file) is 160km from Nairobi, on the outskirts of Kiboko town. A welcome respite from the highway, it is a green oasis and makes a good stop for a cup of chai and some birding. Yellow fever trees surround a freshwater pond fed by the Kiboko Springs, and the garden is lush with shrubs and flowering plants. Look around for **Striated** and **Purple herons, Reed Cormorant, African Darter, Little Sparrowhawk, White-rumped Swift, African Pygmy** and **Giant kingfishers**. Other resident birds include **Green Wood-hoopoe, Crowned Hornbill, White-headed Barbet, Lesser Honeyguide, Retz's Helmetshrike, Wire-tailed Swallow, Red-capped Robin Chat, Black-bellied Sunbird, Spectacled Weaver** and the **Eastern Golden** and **Golden Palm weavers.**

■ *Sagala Lodge:* Turn right at the turn-off to Sagala – 21km after Voi and 7km before Maungu – and drive for 1.5km. Sagala Lodge (http://sagalalodge.com), a private ranch, borders the national park of Tsavo East. Birding in the grounds of this lodge is excellent, and it is a comfortable place to see birds typical of the Tsavo bush.

Among Africa's heaviest birds is the Kori Bustard, which inhabits grasslands below 2,000m.

Peter Usher

Around the bandas there may be bee-eaters, hornbills, barbets and weavers, as well as stunning **Golden-breasted Starling**, **Grey-headed Bushshrike** and (in season) **Eurasian Roller** and **Eurasian Golden Oriole**.

Other birds that come to feed in the garden trees include **Abyssinian Scimitarbill**, **White-crested Helmetshrike**, **Northern Grey Tit**, **Eastern Violet-backed**, **Hunter's**, **Black-bellied** and **Purple-banded sunbirds** and **African Bare-eyed Thrush**.

Golden Palm Weaver

The repeated strains of **Donaldson Smith's Nightjar** fill the night, at the same time that the **Spotted Eagle Owl** emerges. You'll probably see the **Pearl-spotted Owlet** in the daytime, being mobbed by a host of smaller birds. Scores of **Black-faced Sandgrouse** visit the waterhole in the early mornings, while **Vulturine Guineafowl** are daily visitors to the restaurant area and the garden. **Lanner Falcon** and **Eastern Chanting Goshawk** search for prey from the sky.

Taking a drive or guided walk through the *Commiphora* bush on the ranch can turn up **Three-streaked Tchagra**, **Fischer's Starling**, **Golden Pipit**, **Red-billed Quelea** and no fewer than four species of whydah – **Pin-tailed**, **Eastern Paradise**, **Steel-blue** and **Straw-tailed** – which are most recognizable when in breeding plumage. In season there may also be numerous shrikes, warblers and wheatears, **Thrush** and **Common nightingales**, **Irania**, **Rufous Bush Chat** and **Spotted Flycatcher**.

OTHER WILDLIFE

You might see large mammals on the sizeable ranches along the way, although this is not very common from the road.

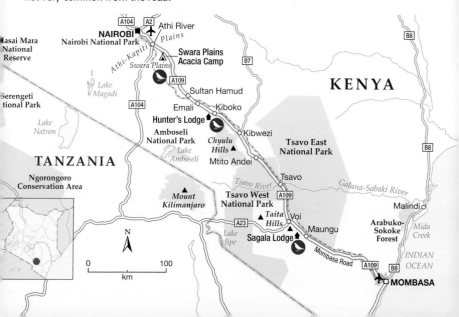

TSAVO WEST NATIONAL PARK IBA

KEY SPECIES
White-headed Vulture, Brown Snake Eagle, Martial Eagle, Somali Bee-eater, Friedmann's Lark, Somali Bunting. **Passage migrants:** Eurasian Roller, River Warbler, Basra Reed Warbler, Olive-tree Warbler, Irania.

At 9,065 km² Tsavo West is large. It comprises miles of grey thornbush and red ochre sands, which are covered with tall, lush green grasses after good rains. It has an equally vast bird list of 600 species, which includes many Palaearctic wintering and passage migrants.

HABITAT
Delonix *Delonix elata*, baobab *Adansonia digitata,* doum palms, euphorbias and other succulents grow in the *Acacia-Commiphora* bush of northeastern Tsavo. In the west of the park, there are the clear pools of Mzima Springs. Their waters originate as rainfall in the forested Chyulu Hills north of Tsavo, and percolate through the rock for many kilometres. The Tsavo River flowing across the northern part of the park also has doum palms fringing its banks, as well as *Acacia elatior* and yellow fever trees *Acacia xanthophloea*. The hills of Ngulia are wooded, while savanna grasslands dominate the south. In the southwest there is the beautiful Lake Jipe (Site 49). Poacher's Lookout is a good place to stop for sweeping views.

GETTING THERE
The Mtito Andei Gate is 245km from Nairobi (250km north of Mombasa), off the busy Mombasa Road (A109); look for a park signpost at Mtito Andei town. Tsavo Gate is almost 50km further along Mombasa Road (before the Tsavo River).

VISITOR INFO
Kenya Wildlife Service manages the park and an entry fee is payable. At Mzima Springs there are walking trails and an underwater viewing chamber where you can see fish and hippos, but be cautious, as there are crocodiles. Tsetse fly may be a nuisance.

A ringing project has been under way here (at Ngulia Lodge) for the past 40 years. It is supported by the Bird Committee of Nature Kenya and takes place during November and December each year. This much-anticipated event brings ringers from many countries and takes advantage of the fact that on most days a low mist layer forms on the Ndawe Escarpment. In these conditions the lights of the Ngulia Safari Lodge attract migrating Palaearctic passerines, sometimes in their thousands, which are then caught in mist nets and ringed.

Peter Steward

A view of the arid Tsavo bushlands with the Chyulu Hills in the distance

THE BIRDING

Driving through the bush and scrub of Tsavo you are certain to encounter the brilliantly coloured **Lilac-breasted Roller**, the charming **Little Bee-eater**, **Red-winged**, **Flappet**, **Fawn-coloured** and **Pink-breasted** larks calling in flight and from perches, and, moving quickly between the trees, the large **Golden-breasted Starling**.

In more open areas in the southeast, **Somali Bee-eater** is often seen hawking for insects. The rare **Friedmann's Lark** occasionally appears and is best distinguished from the very similar **Singing Bush Lark**, which is also found here, by its repeated, loud, single-noted 'wee-oo' call.

As you pass larger trees, be on the lookout for the diminutive **Pygmy Falcon** and larger raptors like **Lanner Falcon**, **Eastern Chanting Goshawk**, **Grasshopper Buzzard** (an Afrotropic migrant) and **Tawny Eagle**. You may also spot **African Grey**, **Red-billed** and **Von der Decken's hornbills**, their distinctive calls giving them away, as well as **Wattled** and **Fischer's starlings**, groups of **Chestnut Weaver** and squeaky **Red-billed** and **White-headed buffalo weavers**.

White-headed Buffalo Weaver

Other bushland residents that you can expect to encounter are **Striped Kingfisher, Pygmy Batis, Rosy-patched** and **Red-naped bushshrikes, Taita Fiscal, Pringle's Puffback, Rattling, Ashy** and **Tiny cisticolas, Grey Wren Warbler, Yellow-bellied Eremomela** and the Afrotropic migrant **Golden Pipit. Eastern Violet-backed, Hunter's, Amethyst** and **Black-bellied sunbirds** are easiest to see at the lodges and camps. Small flocks of **Black-capped Social Weaver** stop and go between the trees, while **Somali Bunting** feed on the ground with other seedeaters, among them the uncommon **Jameson's Firefinch** and **Purple Indigobird.**

Migrant passerines ringed on passage at Ngulia in November and December include great numbers of **Marsh Warbler, Common Whitethroat** and **Thrush Nightingale,** while **River, Basra Reed** (endangered), **Olive-tree** and **Willow** warblers, **Red-backed** and **Isabelline shrikes** and **Irania** may also come to ground at the lodge in remarkable numbers.

Other common migrant visitors to Tsavo include **Eurasian Roller, Eurasian Golden Oriole, Rufous Bush Chat, Eastern Olivaceous** and **Upcher's warblers, Isabelline** and **Pied wheatears, Spotted Flycatcher** and, in April, **Lesser Grey Shrike** and **Sedge Warbler.** The threatened **Corncrake,** while uncommon, is flushed on occasion.

Violet Wood-hoopoe

Lodges and camps are also good places in which to settle yourself and observe the spectacular displays of raptors. On any given day eagles dominate – look for **Black-chested Snake, Brown Snake, Steppe, Wahlberg's, African Hawk, Booted, Martial** and **Long-crested eagles. Amur Falcon** can form spectacular gatherings in the bush when passing through from late November to early December. **White-headed** and **Rüppell's vultures,** both critically endangered, can be seen soaring with the thermals, and the sight of a pair of **Bateleur** in free-fall courtship display is a breathtaking treat.

Male (left) and female (right) Bateleurs

At night, listen out for the call of the **African Scops Owl** and keep watch for nightjars, among them **Eurasian** (in season), **Dusky** and **Donaldson Smith's nightjars** and the Afrotropic migrant **Plain Nightjar**, playing hide-and-seek with insects attracted to lamps.

■ *Mzima Springs:* Visit Mzima Springs in the early morning before the vans of non-birding visitors arrive. The springs are fringed with palms, yellow fever trees and *Syzygium guineense*, with its lovely white flowers. Look out for **Wahlberg's Honeybird** in the trees and **Violet Wood-hoopoe** in the palms. You can also get good views across the water and may spot **African Darter**, **Little Bittern**, **Striated Heron** and **Black Crake**, all attracted by the fish in the pools. Kingfishers include the enormous **Giant Kingfisher**.

OTHER WILDLIFE

The game, including rhino, giraffe, eland, oryx, Burchell's zebra and buffalo, is scattered and it may not be immediately obvious that the greater Tsavo area holds a significant population of Kenya's elephants (over 10,000 animals), including the remaining large 'tuskers' of Tsavo. Keep an eye out for leopard tortoise on or near the tracks and for crested porcupine.

Elephants feeding in the bush at Tsavo

TAITA HILLS IBA

KEY SPECIES

Moustached Tinkerbird, **Taita Apalis**, **Taita Thrush**, **Montane White-eye** (an endemic race), Orange Ground Thrush.

Thirteen biodiversity-rich regions make up the Eastern Arc Mountains. Taita Hills, which comprise Sagalla Hill and the massifs of Dabida and Mbololo, are in the northernmost of these regions. Though the hills have been heavily logged and the forests are fragmented, they retain some special flora and fauna, including the endemic African violet *Saintpaulia teitensis*, found at Mbololo. The **Taita Apalis**, **Taita Thrush** and **Montane White-eye** (known as the Taita White-eye) are endemic birds whose numbers have declined with the loss of habitat.

HABITAT

The mountains rise out of the hot semi-arid plains of Tsavo and are prone to frequent fog and rain, as moisture-laden air from the Indian Ocean condenses on reaching the range.

The area is under intense cultivation, and the forests are reduced to just a few fragments that survive on steep slopes and hilltops. The trees here include species such as wild magnolia *Tabernaemontana stapfiana* and *Albizia gummifera*, the endemic millettia *Millettia oblata*, with its beautiful mauve flowers, and many wild date palms *Phoenix reclinata*. Areas of the Taita Hills have also been given over to plantations of eucalyptus, weeping pine and cypress.

Ngangao Forest, in the Dabida Range, which comprises many fragments, is about 120ha (at an altitude of 1,700–2,000m). Mbololo, with an area of 179ha, is the largest forest fragment. It is situated northeast of Ngangao Forest, is more isolated and better preserved, but is difficult to reach.

GETTING THERE

To reach Ngangao Forest, turn off the Mombasa Road (A109) at Voi and onto the Taveta Road (A23). Stay on it for 23km until you reach Mwatate town. At Mwatate Shopping Centre you will turn right onto the C104 road, which ascends 18km to Wundanyi town. This winding road passes through a beautiful landscape of shambas (farm fields) and homes, forests, valleys and massive granite outcrops, with views of the Tsavo plains in the distance.

Cross the bridge just before Wundanyi town and after about 500m you'll reach a T-junction. Head in a northwesterly direction for 4.5km until you reach a crossing, then keep right and wind around the small centre of Makadenyi. The next bend will bring you to the edge of the forest, which is about half a kilometre before another small centre called Maghimbinyi. Turn left at Maghimbinyi to reach the forest camp and guard house.

Cultivated fields adjoining forest fragments in the Taita Hills

Near the entrance to the forest is a guard house where camping is allowed, but you will need to book and pay at the Kenya Forestry Office in Wundanyi. If you prefer not to camp, there are local lodgings, the nearby Taita Rocks Hotel (www.facebook.com/taitarocks) and a research station called TERRA, established by the University of Helsinki (blogs.helsinki.fi/taita-research-station/news/). A community resource centre set up at the forest entrance has several permanent tents and a kitchen for use.

Be prepared for damp and cool conditions in the forest, especially in the rainy season, when it can be tricky trying both to avoid attacks by safari ants and to watch your step on the steep slopes, all while trying to find the birds.

THE BIRDING

The **Montane** (Taita) **White-eye** *Zosterops poliogastrus silvanus* is locally common across the Taita Hills and can be found in pairs or groups on the margins of most forest fragments and in trees on farms. Its large eye-ring and grey belly distinguish it from the **Abyssinian White-eye**, which is also found here. The forest edge is also good for **Tambourine Dove**, **Black-backed Puffback**, **Stripe-cheeked Greenbul**, **African Dusky Flycatcher** and **Olive Sunbird**.

Also look out for **White-necked Raven** and, in the tree canopy, **Sharpe's Starling**. Typical raptors over forest adjacent to farms are **African Goshawk**, **Great Sparrowhawk**, the rare **Mountain Buzzard**, **Lanner Falcon** and **Crowned Eagle**. There have been no recent records of **Taita Falcon**. **Verreaux's Eagle** is seen at the Chawia forest fragment south of Ngangao.

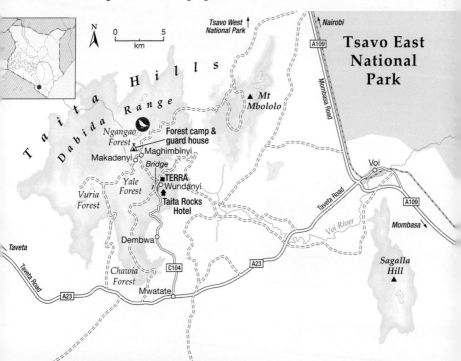

The race is on to secure habitat in the Taita Hills so as to save the Taita Apalis from extinction.

Ngangao is also special for **Taita Apalis,** which may be found low down in forest vegetation, at the edges of streams and on the forest's margins. Listen out for duetting pairs. Also listen for the shy **Taita Thrush.** Although it is more easily found at Mbololo, you may find it foraging in leaf litter on the forest floor, and it has been observed in the lower branches of fruiting trees on the forest edge. Other uncommon species include the **Orange Ground Thrush,** a race of a Tanzanian species that also has a restricted distribution in southeast Kenya, and the resident **Yellow-throated Woodland Warbler,** which has similar southern links.

Moustached Tinkerbird and **Green-backed Twinspot** can be hard to see in the forest undergrowth, but may surprise you at the forest edge in the early morning.

Other typical birds of this habitat are **Lemon Dove, Hartlaub's Turaco, African Wood Owl, Silvery-cheeked Hornbill, Cabanis's Greenbul, Evergreen Forest Warbler, White-starred Robin** and **Eastern Double-collared Sunbird.**

OTHER WILDLIFE

Probably because they are geographically isolated, the Taita Hills are home to an amazing diversity of plants and animals found only here. In addition to the birds already mentioned there are endemic plants, rodents, butterflies, millipedes, snails, caecilians, galagos, geckos and frogs.

White-starred Robin

SITE 49

LAKE JIPE

KEY SPECIES

Great White Egret, Black Heron, African Darter, Straw-tailed Whydah, Taveta Golden Weaver, Fire-fronted Bishop.

The shimmering blue of Lake Jipe occupies the southwestern corner of Tsavo West National Park and extends across the border into Tanzania. It is a shallow lake, about 30km². Many water birds come to feed on the tilapia and *Barbus* fish that swim in this lovely lake.

HABITAT

Streams drain into Lake Jipe from the North Pare Mountains and Mount Kilimanjaro in Tanzania. On the Kenyan side, the lake is thickly edged with *Typha domingesis* reeds, which can tower to over 2m, while pondweeds *Potamogeton* and *Najas* and the invasive water hyacinth *Eichhornia crassipes* can be seen where there are gaps in the reeds at the lake's edge. Owing to increased siltation, water lilies and Pygmy Goose no longer occur here.

GETTING THERE

Follow the directions for Taita Hills (Site 48) as far as Mwatate town, but instead of turning right, go straight through the town and continue for 34km on the Voi–Taveta (A23) Road. Enter the Maktau Gate and go left (south and then southwest) for 48km, following the signs for Lake Jipe. It is also possible to continue past Maktau Gate for 38km to the Ziwani Gate before going south to the lake.

VISITOR INFO

Tsavo West National Park's Jipe Gate is located on the shores of the lake. Here self-catering bandas are available for hire. An entry fee is payable, and you can enquire from the warden at the gate about hiring boats for birding on the

lake. Other options for accommodation include the Lake Jipe Safari Camp (**lakejipesafaricamp.com**), five minutes away, while almost 50km north of the Jipe Gate is the tented Voyager Ziwani Camp (**www.heritage-eastafrica.com/tented-camps/voyager-ziwani/**). Note that lake flies can be a nuisance.

Peter Steward

Whiskered and White-winged Black terns

A gap in the reeds at Lake Jipe

The Squacco Heron wades in wetlands with grass or reeds.

THE BIRDING

The drive to reach Lake Jipe through the open southern grasslands of Tsavo can turn up **Harlequin Quail**, bustards and larks, **Southern Black** and **Pale flycatchers**, the Afrotropic migrant **Golden Pipit** and, in season, **Common Cuckoo** and **Common Rock Thrush**. After rain, check any pools of water for **Water Thick-knee** and, in season, for waders and **Common Snipe**.

There is a wide grassy riparian area leading down to the reeds at the lake. On the lake's edge, fairly close to the gate, is where you'll typically find **African Spoonbill**, **Little Bittern**, herons (including **Squacco**, **Black-headed**, **Goliath**, **Purple** and **Black**), **Great White**, **Yellow-billed** and **Little** egrets and cormorants.

Explore for places where the reeds don't obscure your view, but be careful of herds of elephant coming to drink. These gaps in the reeds at the lake's edge may reveal ducks, **Black Crake**, **Purple Swamphen**, **Lesser Moorhen**, **Red-knobbed Coot** and **Little Rush** and **Lesser Swamp warblers**.

Other birds may include **Whiskered** and **White-winged Black terns**, the stunning **Blue-cheeked** (a Palaearctic migrant, October–April) and **Madagascar bee-eaters** (also a Malagasy migrant, May–September), weavers (the range-restricted **Taveta Golden**, **Lesser Masked** and **Golden-backed**) and **Fire-fronted** and **Zanzibar bishops**. Look for **Black** and **White storks** in season (October–April) and for **Abdim's Stork** (an Afrotropic migrant), which may number in the hundreds after rains. Whydahs (**Pin-tailed**, **Eastern Paradise** and **Straw-tailed**), looking splendid in their breeding plumage, may also be numerous. **African Darter** is known to breed on islands of reeds on the lake.

OTHER WILDLIFE

Oreochromis jipe is a critically endangered endemic fish found only at Lake Jipe, the nearby Lake Chala and the river connecting them.

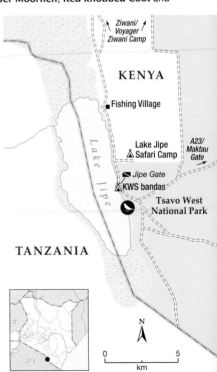

AMBOSELI NATIONAL PARK ⬛IBA

KEY SPECIES

Rufous-bellied Heron, Long-toed Plover, Chestnut-banded Plover, Collared Pratincole, Northern Pied Babbler, Taveta Golden Weaver, Grey Crowned Crane.
Passage migrants: Black-tailed Godwit, Pallid Harrier, Montagu's Harrier.

This stunningly beautiful park, measuring 392km² in area, is situated on the Kenyan plains below the ice-topped peak of Africa's highest mountain, Mount Kilimanjaro. It hosts about 400 bird species.

HABITAT

The two peaks of Kilimanjaro that you can see for miles on the Kenyan side are Kibo (5,895m) and, across the saddle to the left, Mawenzi (5,268m). Both are in Tanzania. There are various different habitats in Amboseli. The area below the mountain is in a rain shadow, and is a rather flat dusty pan with alkaline soils. A third of the park is the dry bed of a 10km-wide soda lake called Lake Amboseli. Its expanse shimmers in the heat and dust devils are common. It fills up seasonally when the rains are good. In contrast to the barren lakebed there are a number of marshes fed by underground springs that draw large numbers of game, including bloats of hippo and herds of elephant that are easy to see on these plains.

GETTING THERE

It is possible to reach Amboseli from the west by way of Namanga town, 162km south of Nairobi, and by then driving east for 73km on the C103 (a rough road) as far as the Meshanani Gate.

Alternately, travel from Nairobi on the Mombasa Road (A109), pass Sultan Hamud and at Emali take the C102 south. Look for the sign to Iremito Gate after 59km and turn right, off the C102, continuing west for 20km on a secondary road. To enter at Kimana Gate, east of the park, don't turn onto the secondary road, but rather continue along the C102. Turn right when you reach the C103, and continue to the gate. The journey from Nairobi currently takes about four hours.

VISITOR INFO

Fees are payable to Kenya Wildlife Service. Don't forget to take some form of identification. It is best to visit when it is sunny, following rainfall, while the wetlands are still full and when migrant waders join the resident water birds (October–April).

With good rains many storks come to feed in the Amboseli grasslands.

Peter Steward

Secretarybirds usually occur in pairs.

THE BIRDING

Approaching from the east, the grassy habitat is dotted with short thorn scrub and a scattering of *Acacia tortilis*. Watch for **Rosy-patched Bushshrike** and **Pangani Longclaw**. The small **Pygmy Falcon** may be on the lookout for prey from a vantage point in a distant tree; a perched **Lilac-breasted Roller** is sure to steal your attention, and numerous **Fischer's Sparrow Lark** will land intermittently on the road. Hornbills are common and **Wattled** and **Fischer's starlings** can be seasonally abundant. Survey the grass for **Secretarybird**, bustards, coursers and **Blue-cheeked** and **Little bee-eaters**.

A track skirts the Enkongo Narok Swamp (by way of a causeway), affording views of **Cattle Egret** piggybacking on wading elephant and **African Jacana** walking on the water lilies in nearby stretches of water. In season, the shallows may be teeming with **Northern Shoveler**, **Northern Pintail**, **Garganey**, **Caspian Plover** and **Black-tailed Godwit** (uncommon). Also look at close range for resident water birds – whistling ducks, **Hottentot Teal**, **Black Crake**, **Red-knobbed Coot** and plovers (**Long-toed**, **Blacksmith**, **Kittlitz's** and the uncommon **Chestnut-banded**).

At the margins of the swamp listen for **Winding Cisticola** and **Little Rush Warbler** and scan for storks, the endangered **Madagascar Pond Heron** (a Malagasy migrant, May–September), **Rufous-bellied Heron**, **Glossy Ibis**, **Collared Pratincole** (which breeds here, April–September) and, in season, **Yellow Wagtail** and numerous waders.

With rains, beautiful **Grey Crowned Crane** and **Saddle-billed Stork** breed here, and in season **White Stork**, which may number in the hundreds, feed in the surrounding grass. In distant pools you may see the shimmering pink of **Lesser Flamingo**. Stop and take a short walk up Observation Hill to catch views of the surrounding swamps and grassland, hippos and **Pink-backed Pelican**.

Back on the tracks, look for confiding families of **Crowned Plover**, which stop to watch as you drive past – also keep an eye out (in season) for shrikes and wheatears.

Flying low in rapid precision there may be **Wire-tailed** and, in season, abundant **Barn swallows** hawking for insects. Likewise numerous **Whiskered** and, in season, **White-winged Black terns** may be moving about over open water, while **Osprey** and harriers work the swamps. Incredible numbers of **Red-billed Quelea** blow over, like wisps of smoke.

A flock of Chestnut Weavers

Other frequently seen birds of prey are vultures, **Amur** (in season) and **Lanner falcons**, **Bateleur**, **Eastern Chanting Goshawk** and **Tawny** and **Martial eagles**.

Woodlands around camps are good birding spots, where it may be easier to observe **Lesser Striped Swallow**, **Northern Pied Babbler**, **African Bare-eyed Thrush**, **Beautiful Sunbird**, **Grey-headed** (Parrot-billed) **Sparrow**, **Yellow-Spotted Petronia** and colonies of **Taveta Golden**, **Lesser Masked**, **Speke's** or **Chestnut weavers**.

OTHER WILDLIFE
Amboseli is a thriving wilderness full of wildlife and it is especially thrilling to watch the large elephant families on these plains.

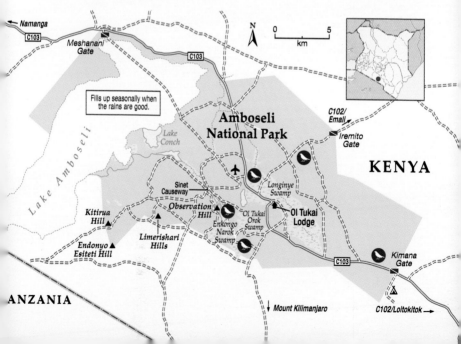

GLOSSARY

The following are some key terms that are used frequently in this book.

abundant of birds that are plentiful, occurring in their hundreds or thousands.

Afrotropic migrant of a bird that travels within the continent and is seen in a given region only at particular times of year.

all-weather road a well-compacted road with no tar or bitumen surface covering.

banda a type of budget accommodation that may or may not have adjoining bathroom facilities. Simple in design, bandas are sometimes round in the manner of a hut.

common of species that are easily found.

endemic of species that occur only in a particular place, for example a bird that occurs only in Kenya.

in season of the time of year when Palaearctic migrants are seen in the country; generally October to April, although some migrants arrive in Kenya as early as September.

lugga describes a river that is usually dry (typically in arid parts of the country) but is expected to fill with water in the rainy season.

Malagasy migrant of a bird that migrates to and from Madagascar.

migrant of birds that travel seasonally from one region to one or more other regions. Certain birds, like Peregrine Falcon, Pied Avocet and Diederik Cuckoo have some populations that migrate and some that do not.

murram road road made from laterite soils that are red in colour and typically consist of very small clay-like rocks (known in some places as gravel)

Palaearctic of birds from Europe or Asia.

Palaearctic migrant of the millions of birds from Europe or Asia that leave their breeding grounds each year and embark on astoundingly long journeys to warmer 'wintering' places, where food is still plentiful.

passage migrant of species that stop briefly in the region on their seasonal migration.

rare/uncommon of species that are few in number.

resident of birds that don't migrate; known to be found at a particular site almost throughout the year, regardless of whether they breed at that site or not.

threatened/endangered at risk of extinction.

REFERENCES AND FURTHER READING

Becker, M., Alvarez, M., Behn, K., Möseler, B. M., Handa, C., Oyieke, H., Misana, S. & Mogha, N. (2014). *Small Wetlands of East Africa, A Field Guide to the Representative Flora*. Bonn: Selbstverlag.

Bennun, L. & Njoroge, P. (1999). *Important Bird Areas in Kenya*. Nairobi: Nature Kenya, East Africa Natural History Society.

Bird Committee, Nature Kenya. (2009). *Checklist of the Birds of Kenya*. (4th ed.) Nairobi: East Africa Natural History Society Bird Committee.

BirdLife International. (2017). Data Zone [online] Available at: www.birdlife.org/datazone/home.

Birnie, A. & Noad, T. (2011). *Trees of Kenya*. Publisher: Authors.

Butynski, T. M. & de Jong, Y. A. (2015). *Laikipia County, Geography, Environment, and Biodiversity*. Nanyuki: Lolldaiga Hills Research Programme, Sustainability Centre Eastern Africa.

Bytebier, B. (2001). *Taita Hills Biodiversity Project Report*. Nairobi: National Museums of Kenya.

Dharani, N. (2006). *Field Guide to Acacias of East Africa*. Cape Town: Struik Publishers.

Gordon, B. & Martins, D. J. (2010). *City Park – the Green Heart of Nairobi*. Nairobi: Friends of City Park, Nature Kenya.

Friends of Nairobi Arboretum. (2012). *Nairobi Arboretum – The Place of Trees*.

Friends of Nairobi National Park. (2012). *Nairobi National Park*. Nairobi: Friends of Nairobi National Park.

Kennedy, A. S. (2014). *Birds of Kenya's Rift Valley*. Princeton: Princeton University Press.

Kenya Indigenous Forest Conservation Programme. (1995). *Arabuko-Sokoke Forest and Mida Creek, the Official Guide*. Nairobi: Kenya Indigenous Forest Conservation Programme.

Laikipia Wildlife Forum (2014). *Laikipia – A Natural History Guide*. Nanyuki: Laikipia Wildlife Forum.

Luke, Q. (2005). Annotated Checklist of the Plants of the Shimba Hills, Kwale District, Kenya. *Journal of East African Natural History* 94(1), 5–120.

Mallalieu, M. (2002). *A Checklist of the Birds of Meru National Park*. Nairobi: Bird Committee, Nature Kenya, East Africa Natural History Society.

Ng'weno, F., Mumbu, D., Ngari, A., Katisho, S., Garama, J., Kenga, S., Jefwa T. and Changawa, P. (2009). *Checklist of the Birds of Dakatcha Woodland*. Nairobi: Nature Kenya, the East Africa Natural History Society.

Ng'weno, F. et al. (2010). *A Checklist of the Birds of Sabaki Estuary*. Nairobi: Bird Committee, Nature Kenya, East Africa Natural History Society.

Pearson, D. J., Backhurst, G. & Jackson, C. (2014). The Study and Ringing of Palaearctic Birds at Ngulia Lodge, Tsavo West National Park, Kenya, 1969–2012: An Overview and Update. *Scopus, Special Supplement* No. 4, the East Africa Natural History Society.

Shanni, I. & De Bruijn, B. (2006). *A Checklist of the Birds of Kakamega Forest*. Nairobi: Bird Committee, Nature Kenya, East Africa Natural History Society.

Shanni, I. (2009). Flying Visitors: The Amazing Phenomenon of Bird Migration. *Kenya Birding* 3, 12–15.

Stevenson, T. & Fanshawe, F. (2002). *Helm Field Guides: Birds of East Africa: Kenya, Tanzania, Uganda, Rwanda, Burundi*. London: T & A. D. Poyser.

Turner, D. A. & Pearson, D. J. (2015). Systematic and Taxonomic Issues Concerning Some East African Bird Species, Notably Those Where Treatment Varies between Authors. *Scopus* 34, 1–23.

Turner, D. A. (2015). Kenya's Endangered Birds and their Habitats. *Kenya Birding* 9, 20–24.

Wagura, L. (2014). *A Guide to Taita Hills' Unique Natural History*. Publisher: Author.

Zimmerman, D. A., Pearson, D. J. & Turner, D. A. (1999). *Helm Field Guides: Birds of Kenya and Northern Tanzania*. London: T & A. D. Poyser.

INDEX TO SCIENTIFIC NAMES

temminckii 66, 78, 79, 84
Calidris alba 131
Camaroptera
  brevicaudata 11
  chloronota 96
Campephaga flava 28, 29, 94, 119, 122
  petiti 96, 99, 100
  quiscalina 46, 113, 114
Campethera abingoni 101, 104
  cailliautii 104
  caroli 96
  mombassica 8, 125, 126, 128
  nubica 68, 71, 85, 88
  taeniolaema 32, 33, 114
Caprimulgus clarus 49, 72, 90, 135
  donaldsoni 72, 141, 145
  europaeus 145
  inornatus 145
  pectoralis 8, 125, 128
  poliocephalus 33
Cecropis abyssinica 26, 29, 49, 62, 64, 82, 153
  daurica 49, 62, 82
  semirufa 110
  senegalensis 42, 44, 84, 96
Centropus chalybeus 104
  monachus 110
  superciliosus 138
Cercococcyx montanus 34
Cercomela familiaris 92, 94, 101, 105
  scotocerca 51, 52, 54, 57, 89, 90
  sordida 37, 38, 44, 79, 115
Cercotrichas galactotes 52, 90, 141, 144
  hartlaubi 21, 22
  leucophrys 71
  quadrivirgata 125, 127
Ceryle rudis 27, 62, 110, 131, 133
Ceuthmochares australis 96, 137
Chalcomitra amethystina 24, 29, 33, 94, 144
  hunteri 46, 60, 94, 141, 145
  rubescens 117
  senegalensis 7, 29, 68, 71, 100, 110
Charadrius asiaticus 54, 56, 104, 152

dubius 46, 49, 66
hiaticula 54, 56, 84, 131
leschenaultii 129, 130, 131
  marginatus 8, 121, 131
  mongolus 129, 130
  pallidus 73, 74, 151, 152
  pecuarius 9, 20, 54, 56, 74, 84, 88, 152
  tricollaris 49, 64, 66, 88, 121
Chlidonias hybrida 31, 62, 64, 84, 111, 112, 149, 153
  leucopterus 56, 62, 74, 84, 88, 106, 107, 110, 111, 112, 122, 149, 153
Chlorocichla flaviventris 22, 59, 128, 137
  laetissima 96, 100, 105, 114
Chloropicus namaquus 45, 46, 62
Chroicocephalus
  cirrocephalus 9, 56, 74, 84
  genei 56
  ridibundus 78, 79
Chrysococcyx caprius 64, 71, 90, 94
  cupreus 22, 26, 39, 96
  klaas 26, 138
Cichladusa guttata 49, 71, 76, 122
Ciconia abdimii 64, 69, 112, 150
  ciconia 64, 69, 150, 152
  episcopus 131, 135
  nigra 20, 69, 150
Cinnyricinclus
  leucogaster 41, 94, 104, 125
Cinnyris bifasciatus 105, 122, 124, 131, 141
  chalcomelas 122
  chloropygius 107, 110
  cupreus 108, 110
  erythrocerca 106, 107, 108, 110
  habessinicus 49, 60, 119
  mariquensis 46, 62, 68, 94, 119, 139
  mediocris 38, 41, 43, 148

nectarinioides 49, 58, 60, 139, 140, 141, 144
  pulchellus 67, 68, 88, 94, 153
  reichenowi 33, 38, 43, 96, 100, 115
  venustus 11, 29, 68
Circaetus beaudouini 111, 112
  cinerascens 95, 96, 101, 104, 110, 111, 112
  cinereus 69, 142, 144
  fasciolatus 126, 128, 136, 138
  pectoralis 59, 135, 144
Circus aeruginosus 31, 36, 57, 64, 82, 122
  macrourus 31, 36, 50, 86, 88, 151
  pygargus 36, 46, 57, 82, 151
  ranivorus 46, 104
Cisticola aberdare 37, 38
  aberrans 101, 105
  angusticauda 101, 103
  aridulus 20, 53, 75, 77, 103
  bodessa 47, 48, 94
  brachypterus 18, 20, 103, 138
  brunnescens 20, 103
  cantans 9, 22, 29
  carruthersi 106, 107, 108, 110
  chiniana 48, 62, 69, 103, 138, 144
  chubbi 100, 115
  cinereolus 53, 67, 69, 70, 71, 144
  erythrops 103
  eximius 103
  galactotes 66, 103, 152
  hunteri 36, 39, 42, 43, 113, 115
  juncidis 20, 77, 103
  lais 67, 68
  nana 53, 69, 70, 71, 144
  natalensis 103, 136, 138
  robustus 20, 35, 36, 66, 103
  tinniens 35, 36
  woosnami 101, 105
Clamator glandarius 45, 46, 90, 94, 117
  jacobinus 46, 90
  levaillantii 102
Clanga clanga 82, 84
  pomarina 105

Coccopygia quartinia 38, 44
Colius leucocephalus 45, 46, 51, 52
  striatus 11
Columba arquatrix 34, 44
  delegorguei 34
  guinea 62, 93
  larvata 33, 148
Coracias abyssinicus 54, 56, 57
  caudatus 7, 8, 119, 143, 152
  garrulus 59, 141, 142, 144
  naevius 46, 68, 71, 88, 94
Coracina caesia 114
Corvinella corvina 118, 119
Corvus albicollis 68, 105, 115, 147
  albus 11, 24
  capensis 9, 31, 36
  edithae 56
  rhipidurus 47, 49, 56, 90, 92, 93, 119
  splendens 133, 134
Corythaeola cristata 95, 96, 99, 100
Corythaixoides
  leucogaster 57, 71, 91, 94
  personatus 76, 77, 101, 104, 107
Corythornis cristatus 24, 27, 49, 62, 66, 110, 133, 134, 135
Cossypha caffra 29, 34
  cyanocampter 97, 100
  natalensis 60, 62, 105, 127, 139, 140
  niveicapilla 97
  polioptera 105, 115, 116, 117
  semirufa 24, 29, 34, 41
Coturnix coturnix 36
  delegorguei 20, 115, 150
Creatophora cinerea 64, 110, 143, 152
Crex crex 77, 144
Crinifer zonurus 107, 116, 117, 118, 119
Crithagra buchanani 67, 68, 71, 88
  dorsostriatus 49, 69, 71
  koliensis 106, 107, 108, 110

INDEX TO COMMON NAMES

Bold page numbers denote photographs.